speakout

Upper Intermediate
Flexi Students' Book 2

with DVD-ROM and MyEnglishLab

2ND
EDITION

BBC

CONTENTS

CONTENTS

THE TIME OF MY LIFE p68 FUTURE ME p71 SO WHAT YOU'RE SAYING IS ... p74 HOW TO LIVE TO 101 p76

**BBC
INTERVIEWS**

What was the best
period of your life?

6.1)) THE TIME OF MY LIFE

G modal verbs and related phrases
P connected speech: elision
V age; word-building: prefixes

SPEAKING

1 Work in pairs and discuss. What are the advantages and disadvantages of being the ages in the box?

| 10 | 15 | 20 | 30 | 45 | 65 |

VOCABULARY

AGE

2 A Match the words/phrases in bold in questions 1–8 with meanings a)–h).

1 If someone looks young **for their age**, is that good? *f*
2 When is someone **in their prime**?
3 If you tell a twenty-five-year-old person, '**Act your age!**' what kind of thing might they be doing?
4 At what age do people generally **come of age** in your country: seventeen, eighteen, twenty-one?
5 Are eighteen-year-olds too **immature** for university?
6 At what age does a person have the **maturity** to make a decision about marriage or a career?
7 At what age is a person **elderly**?
8 Does **age discrimination** affect people looking for jobs in your country?

a) behave in a more adult way
b) 'old' (said in a more polite way)
c) in the best period of their life
d) treating people unfairly based on age
e) reach the age when legally an adult
f) in relation to how old they are
g) wisdom that comes with age
h) childish

B Choose three questions that interest you from Exercise 2A and discuss them in pairs.

READING

3 A Work in pairs and discuss. What do you think it means to 'peak early' or to be a 'late bloomer'? Read the first two paragraphs of the article and check.

B Work in pairs and discuss the questions. Make notes on your ideas.

1 In the photographs, who do you think are late bloomers? Who peaked early?
2 In which of these fields is someone more likely to peak early: acting, singing, writing, sports, business?
3 One author says that sometimes a late bloomer seems to be a failure. Why do you think this is?
4 How do these change as one gets older: freedom, obligation, expectations? What is an example of each?

C Read the article and check your ideas.

EARLY PEAKERS AND LATE BLOOMERS: WHO HAS IT WORSE?

We're all familiar with the story of the film star or singer who peaks early, finds fame at a young age and then seems to disappear. Or the novelist whose brilliant debut at age 22 is followed by works of increasing **mediocrity**. Sports are particularly **biased** towards youth; how many teenagers have a moment of glory at the Olympics only to fade away in their 20s when they are no longer able to compete?

And then there are the late bloomers, who discover their talent relatively late in life: the actress who gets her first big part in her 40s, the office clerk who **pens** a bestseller at 50, and the businessman who starts a multi-million dollar **enterprise** in his 60s. Late bloomers might spend decades struggling to find their passion or be noticed, and that can be painful. As author Malcolm Gladwell wrote, 'On the road to great achievement, the late bloomer will resemble a failure.'

Wherever in the world you are born, society sets out a timeline for your life. You start out confronted by rules and restrictions: you mustn't cross at the red light; don't talk back to the teacher. There are **milestones** of freedom: the age at which your mother says you can stay out late, the point at which you're allowed to take public transport alone or to drive a car. Later, the fruits of your work give you other freedoms, for example you don't have to worry about money for a nice holiday or a meal at a fancy restaurant. And there are the **ever-shifting** sands of obligation and expectations. A teenager complains because her parents make her do her homework and don't let her stay out after 10 o'clock. The 30-year-old suffers because he's supposed to be earning more than his **peers** but he isn't; he has to work all hours but can't find himself in his profession, and meanwhile feels he should give everyone the impression that he's successful even if he isn't.

Early peakers and late bloomers have all made a name for themselves because in some way they managed to break out of the timeline that society had set for them. Perhaps we can all take a lesson from them and break out of our own timeline.

Director Ang Lee had his first global breakthrough at the age of 41 with *Sense and Sensibility* in 1995. Since then, with films like *Brokeback Mountain* and *Life of Pi*, he has become a worldwide success.

After working as a firefighter and insurance salesman, Colonel Sanders was 62 years old when he opened the first Kentucky Fried Chicken restaurant. When he sold the chain in 1964, there were 900 of them.

Wang Yani is a Chinese child prodigy whose work was first exhibited in China when she was four and later became a stamp. Her work now appears in galleries internationally.

It was in 1605, after a career as a soldier and then a tax collector, that Cervantes' novel *Don Quixote* was published, destined to become one of the greatest novels of all time. He was 58.

Romanian Nadia Comăneci, winner of three Olympic gold medals, was the first female gymnast to be awarded a perfect score of 10 in an Olympic gymnastic event. She was only 14. She retired at the age of 23.

As a child, Jocelyn Lavin was a natural mathematician and a gifted oboe and piano player. She later discovered she lacked the discipline for university work and eventually became a teacher.

4 A Work in pairs. Guess the meanings of the words in bold in the text.

B Check your ideas. Match meanings 1–7 with the words in bold.

1 a company or business
2 constantly changing
3 important events in the development of something
4 average quality
5 supporting one group in an unfair way
6 writes
7 people who are the same age or have the same job as you

C Work in pairs and discuss.

- What timeline and milestones do you think society sets out for you?
- Do you feel pressured by this, or is it not a problem for you?

I think I'll be expected to … People tend to … It bothers me that …

GRAMMAR

MODAL VERBS AND RELATED PHRASES

5 A Check what you know. Complete the table with the modal and semi-modal verbs underlined in sentences 1–6 below.

1 You <u>mustn't</u> cross at the red light.
2 Your mother says you <u>can</u> stay out late.
3 You <u>don't have to</u> worry about money for a nice holiday.
4 He <u>has to</u> work all hours.
5 He <u>can't</u> find himself in his profession.
6 He feels he <u>should</u> give everyone the impression that he's successful.

RULES				
obligation (strong)	_____	prohibition	*mustn't*
obligation (weak)	_____	permission	_____
lack of obligation	_____	ability/lack of ability	_____

B Look at the phrases in bold and think about their meanings. Which category in the table are they closest to?

1 They **are** no longer **able to** compete.
2 There are milestones of freedom: … the point when you **are allowed to** take public transport alone …
3 A teenager complains because her parents **make her do** her homework and don't **let her stay** out after 10 o'clock.
4 The 30-year-old suffers because he**'s supposed to** be earning more than his peers …
5 … they **managed to** break out of the timeline that society had set for them.

6 A ▶ 6.1 Listen and write the sentences you hear.

B CONNECTED SPEECH: elision Cross out a *t* or a *d* that isn't pronounced at the end of a word in each sentence. Then listen again and repeat.

We mus̶t go home now.

▷ page 128 **LANGUAGEBANK**

7 A Complete the sentences with a modal verb or related phrase in the correct form. In some cases there is more than one possibility.

1 Parents _____should_____ be strict with babies or they _____ to control them later.
2 The worst thing about school was that I _____ do what I wanted to.
3 When I was a child, my parents often _____ me stay over at my friends' houses.
4 When I was younger, I _____ help clean our flat but I never did.
5 The best thing about being an adult is that no one can _____ you do something if you don't want to.
6 And the worst thing is that you just _____ to get the flat tidy and then the family messes it up again!
7 When I am older I _____ afford an apartment in the city centre.
8 A good thing about being retired is that you _____ work anymore.

B Choose four sentences and change them to give your opinion. Then discuss with a partner.

SPEAKING

8 A Make notes on your answers to questions 1–3.

1 Are most of the people you spend time with your age or a different age? Why?
2 How is your generation different from older or younger ones? What sort of misunderstandings or conflicts can this cause?
3 Is the 'generation gap' greater or smaller than it used to be? Why?

B Work in groups and discuss the questions.

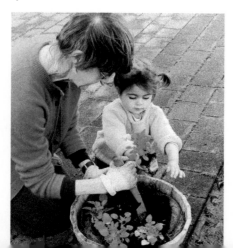

VOCABULARY PLUS
WORD-BUILDING: PREFIXES

9 A Check what you know. Add a negative prefix to the words in bold to make them negative. Use *dis-, in-, il-, im-, ir-, mis-* or *un-*.

1 You have __un__**realistic** expectations of life.
2 Your behaviour is ____**predictable** and sometimes ____**logical**.
3 You are ____**satisfied** with how your life has turned out.
4 You aren't very keen on ____**familiar** situations.
5 You are ____**patient** with people who don't understand technology.
6 You think you are ____**mortal**.
7 You are ____**willing** to change your mind about your opinions.
8 You ____**behave** to get people's attention.
9 You sometimes feel ____**secure** in groups and ____**interpret** what people say to you.
10 How much money you have is ____**relevant**. You're just happy not to be ____**healthy**.

B ▶ **6.2** Listen and check your answers to Exercise 9A. Then listen and repeat. Are the prefixes stressed or unstressed?

C Work in pairs and discuss. Are any of the sentences above truer for younger people and/or older people? Give examples to support your ideas.

speakout TIP

A dictionary can help you find which negative prefix a word takes. Look at this listing below for the adjective *mature*. How is the negative shown? How does your dictionary show negative prefixes?

> **M** **mature** *adj* **1** behaving in a reasonable way like an adult [≠ immature] *She's very mature for her age.*

From Longman Active Study Dictionary.

10 A Answer each pair of questions with words that share the same prefix. Use the prefixes in the box and the words in bold to help.

over- post- pre- under-

What do you call:
1 a) the generation who were born before the **war**? (adj)
   b) the period of **history** before written records? (adj)
2 a) the generation born after the **war**? (adj)
   b) a university course taken after you **graduate** from your initial course? (adj)
3 a) the **time** you spend working in your job in addition to your normal working hours? (n)
   b) people who are forced to **work** too much or too hard? (adj)
4 a) someone who isn't the minimum **age** to see an X-certificate film? (adj)
   b) someone who doesn't have enough **qualifications** to get a job? (adj)

B Work with other students and brainstorm other words that begin with these four prefixes. Which group came up with the longest list?

▷ page 138 **VOCABULARYBANK**

FUTURE ME

G future perfect and continuous
P weak forms: auxiliaries
V optimism/pessimism

((**6.2**

LISTENING

1 A Over the next four years, what are you definitely going to do, what do you think you might do and what do you hope you'll do?

B Work in pairs and compare your ideas. Do you have any plans or hopes in common?

2 Read the programme information below and answer the questions.

1 How does the website work?
2 Do you think it would be uplifting or depressing to get a letter from your younger self?

Letters to myself

The idea is simple:

write a letter to yourself, and futureme.org will keep it and send it back to you at a point in the future – you pick the date. What will you discover, looking back? In this BBC radio programme, people read aloud and comment on their letters.

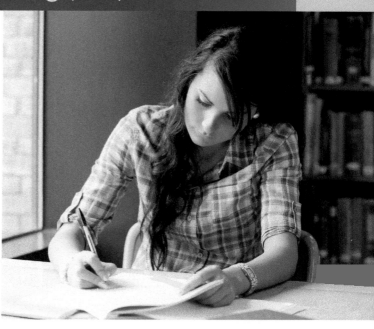

3 A ▶ 6.3 Listen to Laura reading a letter she wrote to herself four years ago when she was sixteen. Answer the questions.

1 Which topics did she write about?
2 Is the letter down-to-earth or romantic? Is it generally optimistic or pessimistic?

B Listen again and correct the mistakes.

1 I envisage myself at Oxford Uni, ... sitting under a tree ... and watching something floaty.
2 I know, I'm practical. I hope that hasn't changed.
3 I hope I'll have married someone.
4 ... I think I'll have three children with long brown hair and blue eyes.
5 ... I have to write everything I can down, but I'm running out of time.
6 Don't worry too much, and be happy with who you are.

C ▶ 6.4 Listen to the second part of the programme and underline the two correct alternatives.

1 Laura now sees her sixteen-year-old self as *shallow/quite mature/unrealistic*.
2 She feels *very happy/ecstatic/amazed* at the way her life has turned out.

GRAMMAR

FUTURE PERFECT AND CONTINUOUS

4 A Look at sentences a) and b) from Laura's letter. Which one talks about:

1 things that will be completed before the moment she opens the letter?
2 things that will be in progress around the moment that she opens the letter?
a) I'll have changed so much.
b) I bet when I get this, it'll be raining.

B Complete the rules.

> **RULES**
>
> 1 To talk about something that will finish before a specific time in the future, use *will* + _____ + _____.
> 2 To talk about something that will be in progress at or around a specific time in the future, use *will* + _____ + _____.

C Underline the correct alternative in the sentences and explain your reason.

1 In ten years' time, I expect *I'll be owning/I'll own* a flat.
2 I'll have finished the report *by/until* 12 and certainly no later than that.

D ▶ 6.5 WEAK FORMS: auxiliaries Listen and write the sentences. Underline examples of the future perfect and future continuous. Circle the auxiliary verbs.

E Listen again and say the sentences at the same time as the speaker.

▷ page 128 **LANGUAGEBANK**

5 A Look back at the rules on page 71 and complete the questions with the correct form of the future perfect, future continuous or the future with *will*.

1 By the end of the day, do you think _____ (you/ receive) more than fifty emails?

2 At 9p.m. tonight, _____ (you/watch) TV? If so, what?

3 Do you think _____ (you/fall) asleep by midnight tonight?

4 This time next year, _____ (you/still/study) English and _____ (you/pass) any English exams?

5 Do you expect _____ (you/still/like) the same kind of music a few years from now?

6 In twenty years' time, _____ (you/live) in the same town, do you think?

B Work in pairs and discuss the questions in Exercise 5A. Use words and phrases from the box.

Possibly   Yes, definitely
That's quite likely   I doubt it
No, definitely not   Perhaps
I expect so   I don't suppose so

SPEAKING

6 A Work alone and think about your plans for ten years' time. Make notes on three of the areas below.

studies or work   *achievements*

travel   **English**

relationships and/or family

home   *activities/experiences*

B Work with a partner and discuss your ideas.

A: *What would you say about 'achievements'?*

B: *Well, in ten years' time, I hope I'll have become fluent in English. I'd like to be working abroad somewhere, maybe Australia. How about you?*

C Work in pairs. Would you say you are generally an optimistic, 'glass half full' type of person or a pessimistic 'glass half empty' one? Give examples.

Glass half full or half empty?

1 How do you feel about your English?
a) It's going well.
b) You **have your ups and downs**.
c) You're stuck and **going nowhere**.

2 This weekend, you're going to a party with lots of people you don't know. How do you feel?
a) You're **looking forward to** it.
b) You **have mixed feelings about** it.
c) It's the last thing you feel like doing.

3 Your partner rings you and asks to meet as soon as possible as they have something important to tell you. What do you think?
a) You **look on the bright side**; the news will be good.
b) It'll just be news, nothing particularly positive or negative.
c) You're **dreading** it; you're sure they want to break up with you.

4 When you think about the next year or two in your life, how do you feel?
a) quite **upbeat** about it
b) cautiously hopeful
c) quite pessimistic about the prospects

5 How does the future in general make you feel?
a) It fills you with great hope.
b) It has its fair share of positive and negative prospects.
c) It **fills you with despair**.

VOCABULARY

OPTIMISM/PESSIMISM

7 A Work in pairs and read the quiz. Guess the meaning of the words/phrases in bold.

B Match the phrases in bold in the quiz with the meanings below. Put the phrase in the infinitive.

1 feel both positive *and* negative about something
2 think about a future event and feel good about it
3 sometimes go well and sometimes go badly
4 make no progress
5 be really worried and fearful about something
6 makes you feel extremely negative
7 optimistic
8 see things in a positive way

C Work in pairs and complete the quiz questions. Then read the key on page 143 and work out your partner's score. Do you think the analysis is accurate?

▷ page 138 **VOCABULARYBANK**

WRITING

AN INFORMAL EMAIL; LEARN TO FOCUS ON INFORMAL STYLE

8 A Imagine you could go anywhere and do anything you like on holiday next summer. Complete the sentence below, and then compare with other students. Did any of you have the same idea?

In the middle of next summer I'd like to be _____-ing (activity) and _____-ing (activity) in _____ (place).

B Read the email about someone's suggestion for next summer and the email reply from her friend. Does Corinna answer Louise's questions? What do you notice about the style?

Hi Corinna!

I've just heard there's an Irish dance and music festival in Dublin in July. [1]How about coming over to visit me and we can go to it together?

[2]Tickets are already on sale, and I'll get us some as soon as I know you're coming for sure. [3]Check out the festival website (I'll paste the address below) and let me know which concerts you'd like to see.

[4]My cousin has a flat in Dublin – how about if we stay there? His family will have left for their summer holiday so it'll be just us staying there. Is there anything else you'd like to do in or around Dublin while you're over here?

[5]Let me know how many days you can stay. Can't wait to see you!

Louise

Dear Louise,

[6]I was **delighted to receive** your email **regarding** the music festival, and **I would like to accept the invitation**. I have always wanted to visit Dublin, and this seems like **the perfect occasion to do so**.

You asked me about concert choices but I didn't get the link. [7]**I would be most grateful** if you could send it again. [8]**My preference would be for** dance rather than music. **I will inform you** of my specific choices once I see the programme.

Your cousin's flat sounds excellent. [9]**I would be interested to know** if it is in the city centre or on the outskirts.

[10]I'll be able to stay for three days, and I will book a flight once I know the concert dates. **I look forward to receiving further information** about it all.

Yours sincerely,

Corinna

C Read the emails again and write the number of the sentence next to the functions below. One sentence has two functions.

a) acknowledge email
b) request information (x4)
c) invite someone *1*
d) accept an invitation
e) make a suggestion
f) providing information (x3)

9 A Read Corinna's reply again. Work in pairs and discuss how to replace the formal phrases in bold with informal ones.

B Complete the table with the phrases in bold.

informal	formal
1 a great time for it	*the perfect occasion to do so*
2 about	
3 Can't wait to hear more	
4 Do you know	
5 happy to get	
6 I'd love to come	
7 I'd rather see	
8 All the best,	
9 I'll let you know	
10 It'd be great	

C Rewrite Corinna's reply in an informal style.

10 A Read the email extract from a friend. Write an informal reply accepting the invitation in 120–180 words.

I'm glad to hear that you're coming next month. This'll be only your second time in this city, won't it?

We could spend Wednesday walking in the hills nearby or perhaps just drive out and look at the scenery. Then would you like to go to the theatre in the evening?

On Thursday some friends of mine are having a party. We could go to that or if you like just stay in and watch a DVD, or walk around town.

Let me know what you prefer. Can't wait to see you!

B Swap your reply with your partner. Check each other's work using the table in Exercise 9B.

C Read other students' replies. Who sounds the most excited about their visit?

VOCABULARY

COLLOCATIONS

1 A Underline the correct alternative.

1 *making/doing* a part-time job
2 *owning/belonging* a smartphone
3 *wearing/putting* make-up
4 *keeping/staying* home alone
5 *getting/making* your ears pierced
6 *going/using* social networking sites
7 *having/signing up* your own credit card
8 *driving/riding* a scooter
9 *babysitting/taking care* for a toddler
10 *journeying/travelling* solo
11 *staying/keeping* up as late as you want
12 *being in charge/running* your own business

B Work in pairs. Which of the activities above can you see in the photos?

C Work in pairs and discuss. What age is appropriate for someone to do activities 1–12?

D Tell the class anything you disagreed about.

FUNCTION

PERSUADING

2 A ▶ 6.6 Listen to a radio phone-in and tick the three activities in Exercise 1A that the people discuss.

B Listen again and make notes about the callers' problems and the DJ's opinions. Then check with a partner.

problem	DJ's opinion

C Work in pairs and discuss. What's your opinion about each of the situations from the phone-in?

3 A Match examples 1–4 with meanings a)–d). Which two are often used to persuade people to agree with you?

1 Is it better to talk it over with her?
2 It's better to talk it over with her.
3 Surely it's better to talk it over with her.
4 Isn't it better to talk it over with her?

a) an opinion
b) a genuine question – the listener can answer *yes* or *no*
c) an opinion where the speaker is inviting the listener to agree with them
d) a strong opinion where the speaker thinks the listener *should* agree with them

B Complete the sentences from the phone-in.

1 _____ up to the parents to set guidelines. (Surely/it/be)
2 _____ it better to talk it over with her? (not/be)
3 _____ just normal nowadays. (Surely/that/be)
4 _____ it's just a stage he's going through? (you/not/think)
5 _____ to be like her friends? (she/simply/not/want)

C ▶ 6.7 Listen and check.

D INTONATION: persuading Listen again and repeat. Copy the intonation pattern.

▷ page 128 **LANGUAGEBANK**

LEARN TO

CLARIFY IDEAS

5 A Read the extract from the radio phone-in. Find two phrases where people ask for clarification of an idea.

DJ: So basically you think she's too young for a phone.

Ed: Yeah, yeah, that's right.

DJ: Surely it's up to the parents to set guidelines.

Ed: So what you're saying is I should give her some rules?

B Read audio script 6.6 on page 148 and find two other phrases to ask for clarification.

speakout TIP

Clarify an idea by repeating something in your own words (paraphrasing). This also 'buys' time while you think about how to react.

C Complete the sentences to paraphrase 1–4.

1 It's unfair. Rich kids don't have to work.
So what you're saying is all kids should ___*have to work*___.

2 Elderly people don't get enough respect from younger people.
So, in other words, younger people should _____.

3 Why is it that students who cheat in exams often don't get punished?
So basically you think students who cheat should _____.

4 It makes me angry that men are paid more than women.
So what you mean is women should _____.

D Work in pairs. Student A: read out a statement from Exercise 5C. Student B: cover the exercise and clarify the idea.

6 A Complete statements 1–4 with your own ideas.

1 The biggest problem with young people today is …

2 It's not fair that …

3 I think it was a mistake to …

4 One thing I learnt from my parents is …

B Work in pairs and swap your sentences. Write a paraphrase of your partner's sentences.

C Work in pairs. Student A: read out your idea. Student B: clarify the idea. Then practise again without looking.

A: The biggest problem with young people today is they can't concentrate.

B: So, what you're saying is they can't focus on just one thing.

A: That's right.

4 A Work in pairs. Do you know anyone who has had a 'gap year' either before they went to university or between university and work? What do you think of the idea?

B Work in pairs and role-play the situation. Use the flow chart to help.

Student A

not / you / think / everyone / a gap year?

Student B

I / not / agree. / not / be / better / start / work as soon as possible?

Yes / but / not / gap year / give people / different kind of experience?

gap year / just / long holiday. Surely / year / work / more useful?

I / disagree. / year off / give / people / chance / think about / career.

not / most 22-year-olds / decide / by that age?

Not always. People / often / end up / job they hate. / Anyway, surely / worth trying?

I / still / not convinced. / I think / a waste of time.

SPEAKING

7 A Work in pairs. For each statement, think of two points that support the opinion and two points against it.

• Thirteen is too young to join a social networking site.

• A sixteen-year-old shouldn't be allowed to get a tattoo.

• An eighteen-year-old who has just passed their driving test isn't ready to drive the family car alone.

B Student A: turn to page 143. Student B: turn to page 144. Student C: turn to page 146.

DVD PREVIEW

1 Work in pairs and discuss the questions.

1 Who is the oldest person you know or have known?

2 What do you think they would say is the secret to a long life?

2 A Match 1–8 with a)–h) to make collocations.

1 keep	a) some gentle exercise
2 follow	b) into monotonous routines
3 do	c) a sensible diet
4 don't fall	d) mentally active
5 avoid	e) a positive attitude
6 stay	f) healthy
7 maintain	g) depressed
8 don't become	h) stress

B Work in pairs and discuss. Which two factors do you think are the most important for a long life?

3 Read the programme information. Which three places are mentioned and what do they have in common?

◁)) Horizon: How to Live to 101

BBC

The quest to live longer has been one of humanity's oldest dreams, but while scientists have been searching, a few isolated communities have stumbled across the answer. On the remote Japanese island of Okinawa, in the Californian town of Loma Linda and in the mountains of Sardinia people live longer than anywhere else on earth.

A group of scientists who study the science of longevity have dedicated their lives to trying to uncover the secrets of these unique communities. Tonight's documentary travels to Okinawa to meet some of its long-living and remarkably healthy inhabitants.

DVD VIEW

4 A Watch the DVD. What are the two main reasons mentioned for why Okinawans live such long lives?

B Work in pairs. What does the underlined word refer to? Watch again and check your ideas.

1 It's four times higher than in Britain and America.

2 The Okinawans don't really think about this.

3 Bradley and Craig think that one of the main reasons for the Okinawans' longevity can be found here.

4 They contain antioxidants, which protect against cell damage.

5 The Okinawans only fill it to 80 percent of its capacity.

6 If you do this, you may die sooner than you might if you didn't do it.

C Watch the DVD again and underline the word you hear.

1 Without thinking about the latest diet or lifestyle *fad/fashion*, Mr Miyagi has developed his own way of slowing the ageing process.

2 The explanation for this extraordinary *phenomenon/miracle* begins in the most ordinary of places.

3 They've identified a number of important *qualities/properties* that protect the Okinawans from disease.

4 You go and you load up at the … at the, the all-you-can-eat restaurant and you, you walk away with this *swollen/bloated* feeling.

D Work in pairs and discuss. How easy do you think you would find it to live on Okinawa? Is there anything you would find difficult?

speakout a debate

5 A Look at the topic for a debate. Work in pairs and write two ideas in favour of the statement and two ideas against it.

Employers should give preference to younger applicants when hiring.

B ▶ 6.8   Listen to part of the debate. Did either speaker mention any of your ideas? Which speaker do you agree with most?

C Listen again and tick the key phrases you hear.

> **KEY PHRASES**
>
> The first point I'd like to make is that …
> I would like to start off by saying that …
> I would like to support the point made by …
> Going back to what [Junko] said …
> I would like to pick up on the point made by …
> In [answer/reply] to the point made by …

6 A As a class, choose one of the topics for a debate.

1   Politicians should be young – younger adults understand the changing world better.
2   Junk food can shorten lives and should be made illegal.
3   Children should take care of their parents when they get old.
4   Workplaces should require employees to do an hour of exercise a day.
5   It's better to live at a very high standard for 50 years than at an average standard for 100.
6   Some younger people think they have nothing to learn from older people, and they're right.

B Work in pairs either for or against the statement. List at least four points to support your opinion.

C Work in groups and debate the topic. At the end, have a vote.

writeback a forum comment

7 A Read the forum comment and discuss in pairs. Do you agree with the writer?

I strongly feel that children should take care of their parents when they get old, and I'm shocked that anyone disagrees. I grew up in a traditional society, where my grandparents lived with us and were always in the house. When I came to this country, it surprised me how unusual it was for three generations to live together. I accept that most young people's lifestyles don't fit with those of grandparents. However, in my opinion, we are fully responsible for taking care of our ageing parents and grandparents. My reasons are that:

- our parents and grandparents invested a lot in caring for us, and it's our duty to do the same for them.
- elderly people can experience loneliness and helplessness. If we care about someone, we should protect them from these feelings.
- it's more expensive and wasteful for people to live in separate homes.

I definitely think that everyone should reconsider the way they live, and move towards a more traditional family structure, even in a modern context.

B Number parts a)–d) in the order they occur in the forum comment.

a) summary statement
b) reasons for opinion
c) statement of opinion
d) personal background

C Choose one of the topics from Exercise 6A and write a forum comment giving your point of view.

D Read other students' forum comments and tell them which parts you agree and disagree with.

V AGE

1 A Add the vowels to complete the sentences.

1 Society, not families, should take care of the _ld_rly.
2 People _n th_ _r pr_m_ should simply enjoy life and not work.
3 The key sign of someone c_m_ng of _g_ is when they earn enough money to pay their own rent.
4 It's embarrassing when an older man or woman dresses too young f_r th_ _r _g_. People should dress and act th_ _r _g_.
5 _g_ d_scr_m_n_t_ _n is necessary in certain types of jobs.
6 M_t_r_ty comes from experience, not from age.

B Work in pairs and discuss. Which sentences do you agree with?

G MODAL VERBS AND RELATED PHRASES

2 A Underline the correct alternatives in the website forum.

★ **My worst job**

My current job is the worst ever. I'm a waiter in an amusement park restaurant and the manager ¹*makes/ lets* us dress up as bears. The costume is the worst and when I'm wearing it I ²*can't/I'm not able* to see properly. I can't believe some of the things children ³*are allowed to/should* do. We ⁴*don't have to/aren't supposed to* get angry with them but I'm sure one day I ⁵*can't/won't be able* to keep my temper and will do something awful! Thankfully, we ⁶*don't have to/ aren't allowed* wear the costumes for more than two hours at a time. Fortunately, because of the masks, my friends ⁷*don't have to/oughtn't to* know about my job. Once, I ⁸*could/managed to* serve two of my friends without them realising it was me!

32 answers • 2 days ago

B Work in pairs and discuss. What's the worst job you've ever had or that you can imagine? What was or would be so bad about it?

G FUTURE PERFECT AND CONTINUOUS

3 A Complete the sentences with the correct form of the words in brackets.

1 Ten minutes from now, I _____ here. (not sit)
2 In two hours' time, the class _____. (definitely finish)
3 By the time you read this, I _____ in New York. I'll be in touch! (arrive)
4 A year from now, all of us in this group _____ regularly. (still communicate)
5 By 2025, the internet _____ by an alternative technology. (replace)

B Work in pairs and discuss. Which of the sentences above are true?

C Work in pairs and write five predictions about yourself/a classmate/a country/a famous person/the world.

D Work with another pair and discuss your ideas.

V OPTIMISM/PESSIMISM

4 A Correct eight mistakes in the words/phrases in bold.

I've **had my downs and ups** at work, but I will never forget my first job: teaching French to a group of sixteen-year-olds in a state school. I **had fixed feelings** about taking the job, since I was very young myself, but I'd learnt to always **look on the light side** of things. I went in the first day feeling **beat-up** and really **looking backward to** meeting my group. But they turned out to be difficult, and for a long time I truly **dread** those lessons. No matter what I tried, I always felt I was **coming nowhere**, and it **filled me up with despair**. Then, one day, something amazing happened. One of the students brought a …

[Comment]

B Work in pairs and discuss. How do you think the story ended?

F PERSUADING

5 A Complete the conversation by adding the missing words from the box to the phrases in bold.

what   surely   isn't   agree
can   clearly   shouldn't

A: Don't you that everyone should be vaccinated against flu?
B: But people ought to be able to choose for themselves.
A: Why? Anyone see that the community needs to be protected and that means everyone has to be vaccinated.
B: But parents decide what they think is best for their children? What about some of the side effects of vaccination?
A: So you're saying is that you think parents know more than the medical profession?
B: But it obvious that it's the companies who make the vaccines that are actually making money?
A: Well, we'll have to agree to disagree.

B Practise the conversation above in pairs. Look only at the phrases in bold to help.

C Work in pairs. Use the phrases in bold in Exercise 5A to discuss the following topics.

1 People who drink and drive should never be allowed to drive again.
2 The ideal world language is _____, not English.
3 Everyone should do one day a week of community service work.

A: Don't you agree that everyone should do community service?
B: Why? Anyone can see that wouldn't be fair …

7 media

TV GLOBETROTTERS p80

THE CAMERA NEVER LIES p83

WHAT'S IN THE NEWS? p86

NEWS BLUNDERS p88

SPEAKING   **7.1** Talk about TV programmes   **7.2** Talk about celebrity and media
7.3 Express strong reactions   **7.4** Retell a news story

LISTENING   **7.2** Listen to an expert talking about hoax photographs   **7.3** Listen to people
talking about recent news stories   **7.4** Watch a BBC programme about live news

READING   **7.1** Read about TV with a global appeal   **7.2** Read an essay on celebrities
and the media   **7.3** Read about tabloid topics

WRITING   **7.2** Write a discursive essay; Use linkers of contrast
7.4 Write a short news article

BBC INTERVIEWS

◀)) What kind of news
stories interest you?

79

G quantifiers
P connected speech: linking
V television; multi-word verbs

NATURAL WORLD

VOCABULARY

TELEVISION

1 A Work in pairs. Think of one similarity and one difference between the TV programmes. Use your dictionary to help if necessary.

1 a wildlife programme – a reality show
2 a costume drama – a soap opera
3 a sketch show – a sitcom
4 a documentary – a docudrama
5 a series – a serial
6 a thriller – a detective series
7 a game show – a quiz
8 a current affairs programme – the news

B Work in pairs and discuss. Which programme types above do you like the most/least? Give some examples.

READING

2 A Work in pairs and look at the photos of five programmes produced in the UK. What type of programme is each one? Why do you think each one is a global hit?

B Read the article and check your ideas.

C Why are sentences 1–8 false? Underline the relevant phrase or sentence in the article.

1 While nature programmes might be expected to be popular worldwide, costume dramas are only popular in the UK.
2 For a car programme, *Top Gear* has surprisingly few cars in it.
3 Viewers loved seeing the bullet train hit the supercar in *Top Gear*.
4 A lot of people thought *The Office* would be successful.
5 *The Office* is actually a serious documentary.
6 Everyone thought that people who liked Sherlock Holmes would welcome a new version.
7 Chinese viewers lost interest in *Sherlock* after the second season.
8 The only dancers on *Strictly Come Dancing* are professionals.

speakout TIP

Good writers use a range of vocabulary to refer to similar ideas, for example *quirky humour* and *slightly strange humour*. This makes a text more interesting for the reader.

D Find words in the article with similar meanings to the following. The numbers in brackets show the paragraph.

1 very good outcome(s) _successes_ (1) _____ (2)
2 mad or unconventional _____ (2) _____ 2)
3 worldwide extraordinary event _____ (2) _____ (3)
4 attracted _____ (2) _____ 4)
5 transmitted _____ (4) _____ (4)
6 brought back to life _____ (5) _____ (5)

E Discuss. Which of the programmes would you most like to watch?

UNLIKELY GLOBAL SUCCESSES

What sort of TV programme would you make if your goal was to appeal to the whole world? Obviously a well-made wildlife programme such as the BBC's *Natural World* series would travel well, with its visual content and cross-cultural appeal. Costume dramas and historical mini-series also seem to survive the transition to a different culture. But how about a car programme, a quirky British comedy or an old-fashioned dance competition? Recent years have seen **quite a few** unlikely successes for programmes with an appeal beyond their intended audience.

Would it surprise you to know that the most downloaded programme ever is *Top Gear*, which regularly attracts over 350 million viewers worldwide in 170 countries **every** week? And yes, we are talking about a car programme headed up by three middle-aged men. True, there are **a large number of** cars, very fast cars, but its appeal lies more in the jokey relationship between the three presenters and also in the crazy challenges that are a key feature of **each** programme. On one occasion, for example, the presenters' bizarre search for the source of the Nile pulled in millions of viewers, and a race between a supercar and a bullet train was **another** huge hit. Like it or loathe it, *Top Gear* truly is a global phenomenon.

THE OFFICE

STRICTLY COME DANCING

SHERLOCK

Comedies rarely travel well and **many** people predicted *The Office* would flop because of its slightly strange British humour. Instead, the American version of the sitcom attracted 11.2 million viewers during its first showing in 2005. Since then, this 'mockumentary' has become an international sensation and has been copied **several** times. The French call it *Le Bureau* while those living in Chile have *La Ofis* and in Germany, it's *Stromberg*. It enjoys **a good deal of** popularity despite the fact that it features characters who aren't particularly funny and survive mundane office life by acting a little cooler than they really are. The boss is a deeply unattractive character who is respected by no one. However, *The Office* is a sitcom with a heart, centred around the romantic relationship between two main characters. Perhaps that's one reason why it has proved such a success.

There are **few** fictional characters as well known as Sherlock Holmes and when the BBC decided to give him a makeover, there was a real risk of alienating fans of the much-loved classic tales. The stories were updated to twenty-first century London, used state-of-the-art graphics and had two relatively unknown actors in the main parts. The BBC now has a worldwide hit on its hands. *Sherlock* is broadcast in more than 200 territories and the long-awaited first episode of the third season was viewed almost seven million times in China only a couple of hours after it was initially aired in the UK. As with *The Office*, people are drawn in by the intriguing relationships between the main characters, so maybe there's a theme developing here. However, this doesn't explain the appeal of our final programme.

Whoever could have imagined that *Come Dancing*, an old-fashioned dance competition popular in the 1960s, would be resurrected as *Strictly Come Dancing* in the UK and *Dancing With the Stars* in over forty-five countries who have bought the format? What's not to like? Show-stopping dances, celebrities, **plenty of** glamorous dresses, big band music, popular hosts and viewer participation, this programme has it all. Celebrity contestants with **little** or **no** experience of dancing pair up with professional dancers and perform in front of a live audience to impress the voting viewers and judges. A tired old format has been revitalised and gone global in a most unexpected way.

It all goes to show that when it comes to picking favourites, the audience will surprise you every time.

TOP GEAR

GRAMMAR

QUANTIFIERS

3 **A** Check what you know. Which of the quantifiers in bold in the article refer to: all; a lot; a moderate or small number/amount; an additional one; zero?

B Complete the rules with the type of noun: *singular*, *plural* or *uncountable*. Use the article to help.

> **RULES**
> **1** Use *several, few, a large number of, quite a few* + _____ noun.
> **2** Use *little, a good deal of* + _____ noun.
> **3** Use *every, each* + _____ noun.
> **4** Use *plenty of, no* + _____ or _____ noun.
> **5** Use *another* + _____ noun.

C In sentences 1–4 below, do the quantifiers *few* and *little* mean *some* or *not many/not much*?

1 There are <u>few</u> fictional characters that are as well known as Sherlock Holmes.

2 There are <u>a few</u> programmes I never miss, perhaps three or four every week.

3 Celebrity contestants with <u>little</u> or no experience of dancing …

4 I always try to spend <u>a little</u> time watching the news each day, at least half an hour.

▷ page 130 **LANGUAGEBANK**

4 **A** ▶ **7.1** Listen and write sentences 1–5 in your notebook.

B **CONNECTED SPEECH: linking** Draw links between final consonants and initial vowels in the quantifiers.

1 All_of_us watch lots_of TV.

C Listen and check. Then listen again and repeat.

5 **A** Find and correct one mistake in each sentence.

1 I watch very little sports programmes.

2 Every programmes have a commercial break every ten minutes.

3 The weekend schedules usually include few talent shows, at least three or four.

4 I like each programmes about hospitals or emergencies.

5 I once spent quite few days watching a box set of the series *24*.

6 I think a large number of TV has been dumbed down.

7 We have plenty detective shows; we don't need more.

8 I think little news is OK but not 24-hour news non-stop.

B Make the sentences true for you or your country.

C Work with other students and compare your answers. How many points do you have in common?

D Report back on three interesting results.

SPEAKING

6 A Work in pairs and discuss the questions.

1 What are the benefits of watching TV online as opposed to on a TV?
2 What types of TV shows do people tend to watch online?
3 What types do you watch online?
4 Would you allow a child online access to a TV or a computer? If not, how would you limit it?

B Work alone. Read the following statements and put a tick (✓) if you agree and a cross (✗) if you disagree.

1 TV and online news is the best way to stay accurately informed about current events.
2 TV programmes and online video hits are a vital part of people's shared cultural experience.
3 Watching TV is bad for you because it robs you of time you might spend exercising.
4 The negative effect of violence in TV programmes and online media is exaggerated. Violent people will do violent things anyway.
5 Watching online video or TV has a negative effect on your concentration span.
6 Sitcoms often provide positive role models for children.

C Talk to other students. Find out how many statements you disagree about. Give reasons.

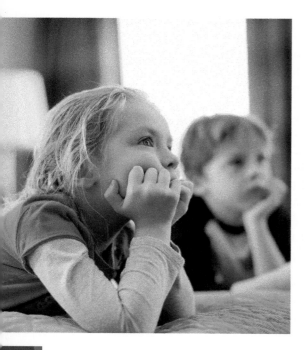

VOCABULARY *PLUS*

MULTI-WORD VERBS

7 A Which programmes in the box might the quotes below come from?

> Natural World   Top Gear   Dancing with the Stars   Sherlock
> The Office   World News

1 'The company has just brought out an electric version of the 408. It's superb! I take back everything I've said about electric models.'
2 'We've just come across a herd of elephants on our way through the jungle. The rain is making it difficult to film but we'll have to put up with it for a few more days.'
3 'Over five hundred turned out to cheer the runners to the finish.'
4 'A marvellous couple! And that dress! It takes me back to my teenage days! And it brings out the colour of your eyes.'
5 'He comes across as a helpful member of the public but it turns out that he's the mastermind behind the crimes. Clever!'
6 'I've lost the key to my flat. Could you put me up for the night?' Otherwise I'll have to sleep at my desk. Like I do most of the day!'

B Underline ten multi-word verbs in quotes 1–6.

C Match meanings 1–10 with the multi-word verbs in Exercise 7A. Add *something* (sth) or *somebody* (sb) in the correct place if the verb takes an object. One verb is a three-part verb.

1 introduce (a product) or make something available   *bring sth out*
2 emphasise, or make something easier to notice
3 tolerate
4 let someone stay in your home for a short time
5 meet by chance
6 seem to have particular qualities
7 make somebody remember
8 accept you were wrong to say something
9 go to watch or be involved in an event
10 happen in the end

8 A Cover the exercises above and complete the sentences.

1 What's one sound, smell or taste that takes you _____ to your childhood?
2 Do you think you come _____ as an extrovert or an introvert?
3 What sort of person do you find it most difficult to put _____ with?
4 Do you always turn _____ to vote in an election?
5 What situation brings _____ the best – and worst – in your English?
6 Imagine you've been dating someone for a year and it turns ____ that they've lied about their age. What would you do?
7 Have you ever come _____ an old friend in an unexpected place?
8 When they brought _____ 3D films, did you think they were worth it?
9 Would you ever put _____ a stranger in your home?
10 If you criticised someone and later found out you were wrong, would you take _____ what you said and apologise?

B Work in pairs. Take turns asking and answering the questions.

▷ page 139 **VOCABULARYBANK**

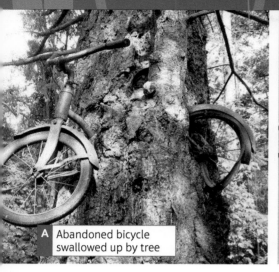

A Abandoned bicycle swallowed up by tree

B Man survives cross-Channel journey in landing gear

C Sharks infest flooded suburban town

LISTENING

1 A Look at photos A–C. Do you think the news events really happened or are they hoaxes?

B ▶ 7.2 Listen to the interview and check.

C Listen again and tick the true statement(s) in each sentence.

1 The guest wants to remain anonymous because
   a) he thinks mystery is important.
   b) he doesn't want to get sued.

2 Police pay him to
   a) work out if a photo is a hoax.
   b) find out who did it.

3 He says the bike photo
   a) is easy to put together from two photos.
   b) was put together by a friend of his.

4 The guest says the plane photo
   a) could be real.
   b) is well done.

5 He laughs at the shark photo because
   a) hoax photos with sharks are common.
   b) this one looks so fake.

6 People who produce hoax photos do it because
   a) they can make good money.
   b) they feel excited when the hoax succeeds.

D Tick the statements you agree with. Then discuss your ideas with a partner.

1 When I see a photo in the media, I assume it's real.

2 It should be illegal to publish hoax photos. It's the same as publishing false news.

3 It's unfair to show a famous person in an embarrassing situation in a hoax photo.

4 It's more fun to be tricked by a hoax photo than to find out that it's fake.

GRAMMAR

REPORTED SPEECH

2 A Check what you know. Which sentences below report a) a statement, b) a request or c) a question?

1 I asked you before the show if you'd ever earned money for your hoax work.

2 A friend told me he had seen it with his own eyes a number of years before.

3 You said that you often work with the police.

4 Sometimes the police ask me to look at it.

B For the sentences in Exercise 2A, write the exact words each person said.

1 'Have you ever earned money for your hoax work?'

C Work in pairs and complete the rules.

> **RULES**
>
> **1** In reported statements and questions the verbs usually shift back if the reporting verb (*say, tell,* etc.) is in the *past/present*.
>
> **2** This doesn't happen in sentence *1/2/3/4* because the reported information is *always true/still true*.
>
> **3** In reported questions the word order is the same as *a question/an affirmative statement*.
>
> **4** To report a request, use *ask somebody* + infinitive with *to/gerund*.

▷ page 130 **LANGUAGEBANK**

3 A Work in pairs. Who says each of these sentences, the presenter (P) or the hoaxer (H)?

1 Can you explain why you want to remain anonymous?

2 What exactly do you do for the police?

3 Talk us through the photographs if you would.

4 I wasn't sure myself, but I found out it was near Seattle, Washington.

5 Is there a technical reason why you know it's a hoax?

6 I'm thrilled when people believe one of my photos.

B Write the sentences in reported speech. Start with *He/She said/asked.*

VOCABULARY
REPORTING VERBS

4 A Read the news story and discuss with a partner. Do you think Les Brown is telling the truth?

Insurance hoax?

An insurance company has accused a Louisville man of faking injuries from an on-the-job accident in order to get a large insurance payment. Les Brown, 49, denies lying to authorities about his injuries, and has promised to prove that photos showing him playing tennis are fake. Brown has refused to speak to journalists about the matter.

B Read the update to the story below. Have you read about any similar stories in the news?

Faced with clear evidence, Les Brown has admitted faking his injuries to cheat the insurance company. His ex-wife persuaded him to stop lying about the situation after authorities warned Brown to tell the truth or face a long jail term. Brown has apologised for embarrassing his family and has agreed to pay a large fine.

C Look again at the texts and underline all the reporting verbs.

D Write each reporting verb next to the pattern that follows it.

1 -*ing* form	
2 preposition + -*ing* form	
3 object + preposition + -*ing* form	*accuse sb of doing sth*
4 infinitive	
5 object + infinitive	

5 A Check what you know. Add the verbs in the box to the table above. If you are not sure, use examples in a dictionary to help.

tell   invite   suggest   advise   remind   threaten   offer

B ▶ 7.3 WORD STRESS Work in pairs. Which reporting verbs in the completed table have the stress on the first and which on the second syllable? Listen and check.

C Complete the sentences so they are negative.
1 He accused them _____ (take) his injuries seriously.
2 He persuaded his doctor _____ (talk) to the media.
3 His wife told him _____ (lie) about the situation.
4 He apologised _____ (tell) the truth.
5 The authorities warned him _____ (do) it again.

6 A Complete the questions with the correct form of the verb in brackets.

Questions of Trust

Situation 1
A colleague has a photo of you at an office party doing something embarrassing. He threatens to show it to your boss unless you pay him a small sum of money. Would you:
a) agree _____ (pay) the money since it's a small amount, just to avoid trouble?
b) deny _____ (do) anything wrong and tell your colleague to do whatever he wants?
c) talk to your boss and apologise _____ (act) stupidly?

Situation 2
Someone shows you a printout of an email written by your best friend. It's full of negative comments about you and also contains a few secrets that you told your friend. Would you:
a) accuse your friend _____ (betray) you?
b) refuse _____ (believe) that the email is real, and do nothing?
c) make your friend admit _____ (write) the original email and warn him/her _____ it again (never do)?

Situation 3
A year ago, you promised to take a friend out to dinner for her birthday at an expensive restaurant. She's just reminded you, but now you don't really have the time or money. Should you:
a) promise _____ (take) her but next year?
b) persuade her _____ (go) to a cheaper restaurant?
c) tell her the situation and apologise _____ (not keep) your promise?

Situation 4
Your boss has offered to give you a bonus if you write a report that will have her name on it and that she will take full credit for. Would you:
a) offer _____ (do) it but only if she gives you credit, too?
b) suggest _____ (ask) someone else?
c) say no and threaten _____ (report) your boss to her boss?

B Work in pairs. Take turns to ask and answer the questions in Exercise 6A.

SPEAKING

7 A Work in pairs. Look at statements 1–4. Choose two statements and write one reason for and one reason against each one. Give examples to support your ideas.

1 Manipulation of images in advertising is justified in order to make a message stronger.
2 Idealised images of models in media can have a positive effect on ordinary people.
3 The media should be free to examine the lives of public figures.
4 The media should focus more on the lives of ordinary people rather than on famous people.

B Work with other students and compare your ideas.

WRITING

A DISCURSIVE ESSAY; LEARN TO USE LINKERS OF CONTRAST

8 A Read the essay and discuss. Which topic in Exercise 7A is it about? Do you agree with the writer's point of view?

These days the media is full of stories of celebrities' private lives: their relationships, rows, problems with weight and so on. In fact, the public seems to have a never-ending appetite for this type of gossip.

It could be argued that celebrities invite publicity despite knowing that this will leave them open to public attention. Therefore, it is hypocritical for them to complain when the media shows interest in other aspects of their lives. Also, celebrities are influential role models to many people and because of this, their private lives should be open to public examination. Additionally, the public have the right to know about the rich and famous since it is our money that supports them.

However, there are several reasons why celebrities deserve a certain level of privacy. Firstly, while some people actively seek fame, others do not. For example, a person might want to be a great tennis player but not wish to suffer media intrusion into their family's private life. Secondly, although reporters might claim an item is 'in the public interest' often, in fact, they are more interested in selling a sensational story. Lastly, the unwelcome attentions of reporters and photographers can put celebrities under great stress.

On balance, I believe that celebrities have the right to the same kind of privacy as anyone else. Just because on some occasions they invite interest in order to publicise their work, this does not mean that they should not be able to say 'no'.

B Read the essay again and underline the correct alternative.

1 The introductory paragraph *explains why the topic is of interest/gives the writer's opinion about the topic*.
2 Paragraph two gives points *for/for and against* the idea.
3 Paragraph three gives points *against/for and against* the idea.
4 The conclusion *asks the reader's/gives the writer's* opinion.

9 A Look at sentences 1–4. Circle the linker which is used to show a contrasting idea.

1 Celebrities invite publicity (despite) knowing that this will leave them open to public attention.
2 While some people seek fame, others never want or plan for it.
3 Although a reporter might claim that a story is 'in the public interest', often they are more interested in selling a sensational story.
4 However, there are a number of reasons why celebrities deserve our sympathy.

B Work in pairs and answer the questions.

1 What punctuation follows *However*?
2 Which form follows *despite*?
3 In sentences 1, 2 and 3, which is the main clause?
4 Do the linkers in 1, 2 and 3 introduce the main clause or the subordinate clause?

C Use the linkers in brackets to connect the ideas in two different ways.

1 some celebrities are good role models for young people / others set a negative example (however, although)
2 anonymously published internet news is unreliable / many people rely on it as a main source of information (despite, while)
3 false reports of celebrity deaths are common / some people still believe them (while, however)
4 the scandal damaged his reputation / he still has millions of fans (although, despite)

10 A Write notes for the four sections of a discursive essay on one of the other topics in Exercise 7A.

B Write the essay (250–300 words).

F adding emphasis
P sentence stress
V the press

VOCABULARY
THE PRESS

1 A What do you think are the most popular topics in newspapers? Read the article below and check your ideas.

Six topics that keep the tabloids in business

In an age when quality newspapers are seeing a serious drop in **circulation**, tabloid journalism is in no danger of dying out. Six topics always guarantee sales:

1 Scandal – the public loves glimpses into the lives of the rich, famous and powerful and scandal fuels **tabloid** sales.

2 Money – everyone wants it, and some people will stop at nothing to get it. Many tabloids have a regular **feature** about money.

3 Babies – whether it's because they were born in a taxi or can speak two languages from birth, it seems we can't get enough of them.

4 Animals – flip through any tabloid and you'll find a heart-warming story about a brave dog, or a cat that's befriended a mouse.

5 Royalty – hardly a day goes by that a 'royal' doesn't make an appearance in a morning **edition**.

6 Winners – from lottery winners to Olympic gold medallists, a winner on the front cover guarantees high sales.

Bold headlines, plenty of appealing photos, a low price and a colour **supplement** or two make tabloids the perfect escape from real life. They aren't afraid to be **biased** and show their opinion, most strikingly in the **editorial page**, which tends to be direct and aggressive in stating the editor's position on major issues. The public want excitement and **sensationalism**, and tabloids deliver.

B Match meanings 1–8 with the words in bold in the article.

1 a popular newspaper, half the size of a standard newspaper, with few serious stories   *tabloid*
2 the section that gives the paper's opinion
3 a special report or article about a topic
4 giving a single point of view, unfairly
5 an extra section of a newspaper which can be pulled out, often a magazine
6 reporting news to make it sound as exciting as possible
7 the set of newspapers which are published at the same time
8 the number of newspapers sold in a day or week

C Work in pairs and discuss the questions.

1 Which paper in your country is the most sensationalist/biased?
2 Which sections of a newspaper or online news do you read first, e.g. sports, etc.?
3 Which sections or stories do you never read?

▷ page 139 **VOCABULARY**BANK

A Shop Clerk Cheats Lottery Winners

B MATCH FIXING SHOCK

FUNCTION
ADDING EMPHASIS

2 A Work in pairs and look at tabloid headlines A–F above. What do you think the stories are about?

B ▶ 7.4   Listen to the conversations. Which headlines do they talk about?

C Listen again. What surprises the woman most in each story?

3 A Work in pairs. Underline the phrases that the speakers use to add emphasis.

1 The amazing thing is that the tiger ran off.
2 Wow, there's no way I'd do that!
3 You're the one who's always telling me to stop.
4 That is so wrong!
5 That's totally outrageous!
6 I do think they should do something about it.
7 That *is* a good idea.
8 How on earth did he catch it?
9 That's such an amazing thing!
10 Absolutely incredible!

B Work in pairs and discuss the questions.

1 What is the difference between *so* and *such*?
2 In sentence 6, what is unusual?
3 In sentences 5 and 10, what other modifiers could be used with the adjectives?
4 How is the beginning of sentence 3 different from 'You're always telling me …'?
5 In sentence 8, what expression is added to a question word to show surprise?

C ▶ 7.5   SENTENCE STRESS Work in pairs and mark the main stresses in the sentences in Exercise 3A. Listen and check. Then listen and repeat.

speakout TIP

The words that show surprise are usually stressed and said with high intonation (pitch). It's a good idea to exaggerate when you practise this to help you get it right.

▷ page 130 **LANGUAGE**BANK

C Baby Saved From Ledge Fall

D Prince takes first steps

E WIFE'S LADLE SAVES MAN FROM TIGER

F POP STAR LOVE TRIANGLE

4 A Rewrite the sentences to add emphasis using the words in brackets and making any other changes necessary.

Conversation 1

A: I'm so/angry with you. Why didn't you tell me about the party? (so)

B: But I told you. A few minutes ago. (did)

A: That's helpful! How am I supposed to get ready in time? (really)

B: But you said you never want to go to parties. (one)

Conversation 2

A: Dave's good-looking but she's crazy about Will. (absolutely)

B: It's sad. Dave adores her. (the sad thing)

A: Yeah, and he's really kind; a nice man. (such)

B: What shall I say if he asks me about Will? (earth)

Conversation 3

A: I'm quitting my job. It's badly paid and it's hard work. (so, such)

B: I think you'll regret it. (do)

A: You always say I should do what I want. (one)

B: But you shouldn't just quit. (no way)

B Work in pairs and add two more sentences to each conversation. Add emphasis to one of your sentences in each conversation.

C Cover and practise the conversations.

LEARN TO
MAKE GUESSES

5 A Work in pairs and try to complete the extract. Then check your ideas in audio script 7.4 on page 149.

A: It's lucky the men noticed the baby.
B: Yeah, I ¹_____ they saw some movement.
A: Or ²_____ they heard something.
B: What's that? The woman's bringing something.
A: It's ³_____ to say but it ⁴_____ like a cushion.
B: Yeah, it ⁵_____ be a sofa cushion.
A: I ⁶_____ they thought the baby might fall on it.
B: That ⁷_____ be the luckiest baby alive.

B Which words in 1–7 above could be replaced by words in the box?

difficult   seems   perhaps   think   might   's surely   imagine

6 A ▶ 7.6 Listen to the sound. What do you think it is? Write down two ideas.

B Use the prompts to discuss the sound.

A: What / you / think / it / be?
B: hard / say / but / might / be (your first idea)
A: think / sound / like (your first idea)
B: suppose / could / be (another idea)
A: Or / perhaps / be (another idea)
B: Well / think / it / be (final decision)

C ▶ 7.7 Listen to five more sounds. Practise the conversation after each one.

SPEAKING

7 A Work in pairs and look at the categories. What do you think the top five are for each category?

The top five …
1 most dangerous animals
2 countries with the tallest people
3 cities for art lovers
4 friendliest countries

A: *I imagine the most dangerous animal is a tiger. What do you think?*
B: *I'm not sure. I suppose it could be, but …*

B Work in groups and take turns. Student A: turn to page 143, Student B: turn to page 144, Student C: turn to page 145, Student D: turn to page 146. Student A: tell the other students your category and see how many items they can guess. Tell them the answers they don't guess. Discuss which answers are the most surprising.

DVD PREVIEW

1 A Work in pairs and discuss the questions.

1 How often do you watch the news? Are the newsreaders in your country always serious?

2 What are the pros and cons of working as a TV newsreader?

3 The name of the programme you're going to watch is *The Funny Side of the News*. What do you think it's about?

B Read the programme information and answer the questions.

1 Why are there more mistakes on TV news than there used to be?

2 How many different types of mistakes are mentioned?

The Funny Side of the News   BBC

The Funny Side of … is a BBC series that looks at all the things that can go wrong on TV, from talent shows to wildlife programmes. Tonight it takes a look at TV news. As serious as news can be, mistakes and **blunders** are unavoidable. And with the introduction of 24-hour **rolling** news, mistakes have become more frequent and more visible with newsreaders **stumbling over their words** and endless **technical hiccups**. From microphones **malfunctioning** to the wrong guest being brought into the studio for an interview, disaster is waiting to **strike** at any moment.

C Look at the programme information again and match the words/phrases in bold with 1–6 below.

1 hesitating or making mistakes when speaking

2 happen suddenly and cause damage

3 small problems with machines

4 continuous

5 mistakes

6 going wrong (for a machine)

DVD VIEW

2 A Watch the DVD and make notes on which blunder:

• you found the funniest.

• you didn't find funny or didn't understand.

B Work in pairs. Number the blunders in the order they appear in the programme. Some have more than one example (there are seven). Then watch the DVD again and check.

Malfunctioning equipment *1*

People stumbling over their words

The wrong guest in an interview

An accident on a live programme

A: There was the bit where the woman …

B: Yes, and there was the part where the guy …

C Complete extracts 1–5 from the DVD. Then watch again and check.

1 So if it starts going _____, you're going to see it.

2 The _____ about rolling news _____ that you have to fill an awful lot of time …

3 I'm afraid we obviously have the wrong guest here. That's deeply _____ for us.

4 But the undisputed _____ of the wrong guest division is the BBC News 24 incident _____ the charming but inappropriate Guy Goma.

5 It goes to _____ just how much the public love a good news blunder.

D Discuss. Which incident do you think was the most embarrassing for the newsreader?

speakout a news story

3 A ▶ **7.8** Listen to someone retelling a news story about a man who swapped a paper clip for a house. Number the things he traded in the correct order.

a paper clip *1*
a snow globe
a pen shaped like a fish
a house
a door knob
a part in a film

B Listen again and tick the phrases you hear.

> **KEY PHRASES**
>
> Did you [hear this story/see the news] about … ?
> I [heard this story/read this article] about …
> Apparently what happened was …
> According to [the report/the guy on the news] …
> Anyway, so he …
> I don't remember all the details, but …
> The [weird/strange/interesting thing] was …

C Think about a recent news story. Make notes listing the events in the story and think about which key phrases you can use.

D Work in groups and tell each other your stories. Ask follow-up questions and take notes. Which story was the most interesting?

writeback a short summary

4 A Read the article and write down the one thing that the man traded that is mentioned in the article but not in the recording.

Man trades paper clip for house

A Canadian man has made headlines by trading a paper clip for a house. Bored blogger Kyle Macdonald started by exchanging small objects – a pen, a door knob, a neon sign – but step by step the 26-year-old built up to items of larger and larger value, and after one year his journey from paper clip owner to homeowner was over.

B Read the article again and do the tasks.

1 Circle three different ways that Kyle Macdonald is referred to in the story apart from *he* or *his*.
2 Underline two places where the writer uses two different words for the same thing.
3 Put a box round two places where a word is repeated. What effect does this have?

C The article is exactly 60 words. Imagine your editor tells you to cut it to exactly 45 words. Which words could you omit without losing important details (hyphenated words count as one word)?

D Write an article of exactly 60 words about one of the stories your group told in Exercise 3D. You may need to invent some details.

E Student A: read your article aloud. Other students: is it a summary of the story you told in Exercise 3D? If so, is it accurate?

Ⓥ TELEVISION

1 A Find fifteen kinds of TV programme in the wordsnake.

sketchshowsitcomthenewscostumedrama
currentaffairsprogrammesoapoperareality
gameshowsgammedocudrama
showcurrentaffairsprogram
detectiveseriesgameshow
documentarydetectiveseriesgameshow
yshowthrillerwildlifeprog
reality

B Work in pairs. Which type of programme would you choose if you wanted to:

- laugh?
- learn something?
- just relax and watch real people?
- catch up on the news?
- test your knowledge?

Ⓖ QUANTIFIERS

2 A Work in pairs and underline the correct alternative. The sentences are about two people.

1 *Both/Few* of us enjoy spending time in airports.
2 *None/Neither* of us plays a musical instrument.
3 We remember *a large amount of/quite a few of* our dreams.
4 Both of us take *a few/a little* sugar in our coffee.
5 We both got *hardly any/very few* sleep last night.
6 *Neither/Both* of us is allergic to anything.
7 We like *all/every* type of music.
8 We would like to live in *other/another* country.
9 We spend *several/a great deal of* hours in the gym every week.
10 We both like having *few/a few* minutes' sleep in the afternoon.

B Which sentences are true for you and your partner? Change any that are not true.

A: Do you enjoy spending time in airports?
B: No.
A: Me neither. OK, so neither of us enjoys spending time in airports.

Ⓖ REPORTED SPEECH

3 A Rewrite the sentences in reported speech.

1 Last week, an interviewer asked me, 'What's your biggest weakness?'
2 The other day, a complete stranger walked up to me and asked, 'What have you been doing lately?'
3 Once, I was trying on trousers and the shop assistant asked, 'Would you like to try a bigger size?'
4 Every day, my flatmate says, 'Could you do the dishes?' and then says, 'I'll do them next time.'
5 At the end of a first date, the girl asked me, 'So when do you want to get married?'
6 At 3a.m., my phone rang, and the caller asked, 'Are you sleeping?'

B Which question would make you feel the most uncomfortable?

Ⓥ REPORTING VERBS

4 A Complete the questions with the correct form of a verb in the box. Add any necessary words.

~~help~~   quit   lend   make
do   pay   be (x2)

1 When was the last time you offered _to help_ someone?
2 Do you find it easy to admit _____ a mistake?
3 Would you ever agree _____ a friend a large amount of money?
4 Have you ever refused _____ a bill?
5 Would you always apologise _____ late?
6 Have you ever threatened _____ your job?
7 Have you ever been accused _____ too serious?
8 Do you often promise _____ something and then simply forget?

B Work in pairs and discuss the questions above.

Ⓕ ADDING EMPHASIS

5 A Find and correct the mistakes. There is one extra word in each sentence.

1 My hometown is such a so boring place.
2 I so do think that some people are very generous.
3 It's totally very ridiculous that people have such short holidays.
4 Why on the earth am I learning English?
5 Really, there's that's no way I would ever borrow money from a friend.
6 My teacher was the one who she had the most influence on me when I was young.
7 Sometimes learning English is so such difficult that I want to give up.
8 I like cooking, but the surprising thing that is that I never do it.

B Work in pairs and take turns. Student A: read one of your sentences from Exercise 5A. Student B: continue the conversation using some of these follow-up questions.

How do you mean?

In what way?

Why (not)?

For example?

What makes you say that?

8 behaviour

IT'S A TOUGH CALL p92

FAIR SHARE p95

HAVE YOU GOT A MINUTE? p98

THE HUMAN ANIMAL p100

BBC INTERVIEWS

What kind of behaviour gets on your nerves?

8.1))) IT'S A TOUGH CALL

G past and mixed conditionals
P connected speech: weak forms
V collocations: decisions; compound adjectives

READING

1 A Work in pairs. Look at the photos and read the headlines. What do you think happened in each situation? Write two predictions about each one.

B Read the articles and check your ideas.

C Look at statements 1–8 below. Who do you think said each one?

1 I'm looking for something to support my family.
Delroy Simmonds

2 Her face wasn't covered so I recognised her immediately.

3 She said, 'I have a lot of money in that couch and I really need it.'

4 I'm incredibly grateful, and my three other kids are too.

5 It was hard for him. I think that's why he came in with his brother.

6 Look, there's something in here.

7 You shouldn't have done that.

8 We laid it all out and we were screaming.

D Work in pairs and discuss. Who had the most difficult decision: the three roommates, Simmonds or McQuinn's father? Do you think you would have behaved in the same way?

2

Man misses job interview to save baby from train

An unemployed Brooklyn man missed a job interview for the best of reasons: He was saving the life of a nine-month-old boy who was blown into the path of an oncoming subway train by a gust of high wind. Like a superhero without a cape, Delroy Simmonds jumped onto the tracks and lifted the bleeding child – still strapped into his stroller – to the safety of the platform as the train bore down on them. 'If he hadn't jumped down there, the baby wouldn't be alive,' said a worker at the station. 'Everybody thinks I'm some sort of superhero,' the father of two said. 'I'm just a normal person. Anybody would have done the same.' A friend of Simmonds thought differently. 'If that had happened to me, I might not have jumped.'

The out-of-work Brooklyn native was on his way to apply for a maintenance position at a warehouse. 'A strong gust of wind blew,' he recalled. 'There was a woman with four kids. One was in a stroller. The wind blew the baby onto the tracks.' He had no time to assess the situation. 'The train was coming around the corner as I lifted the baby from the tracks. I really wasn't thinking.'

1

New York roommates find $40,000 in sofa

Three roommates who bought a used couch for $20 found $40,000 in cash stashed inside and returned the money to the 91-year-old widow who had hidden it there.

Cally Guasti said that she and her friends had bought the beat-up couch and a chair for $55 at a Salvation Army thrift store. They noticed the arm cushions were weirdly lumpy. Then roommate Reese Werkhoven opened a zipper on one arm and found an envelope. It contained $4,000 in bubble-wrapped bills. Guasti, Werkhoven and roommate Lara Russo opened the other arm zipper and started mining the treasure stashed inside. They counted it up: $40,800.

Later on, Guasti found a deposit slip with a woman's name on it, and then phoned her. They drove to the home of the woman, who cried in gratitude when they gave her the cash she had hidden away.

Guasti said the three had considered the option of keeping the money, but decided they couldn't do that. It went against their principles. 'At the end of the day, it wasn't ours,' Guasti said. 'I think if any of us had used it, it would have felt really wrong.'

3

FATHER TURNS IN BANK-ROBBING DAUGHTER

An Adelaide man made the hardest choice of his life this weekend: he turned his own daughter into police after recognising her photo from a police report about a recent string of bank robberies. Neighbour Bill Baugely says the heartbroken dad was trying to protect his daughter. 'It's a really tough situation,' Baugely said, 'But I would have done the same thing.'

Twenty-seven-year-old Anne McQuinn was allegedly seen at the St George Bank in King William Street, at the Suncorp Bank in Grenfell Street, and at a bank in nearby Elizabeth in the past few months. Sergeant Tom Landers of the Adelaide police said, 'The father came into the station with the woman's uncle. They'd seen the photos on TV and the internet, and were sure it was McQuinn.'

Police say the father didn't want to put off the decision once he saw it was his daughter and came in immediately. 'The surveillance photos were clear,' said police. 'He really had no doubt it was her.'

The father said most of his friends were supportive, but not everyone. Local resident Gerry Comber said, 'OK, the guy wants to do the right thing, but who turns in their own daughter?'

VOCABULARY

COLLOCATIONS: DECISIONS

2 A Find verbs in the articles to complete the word webs.

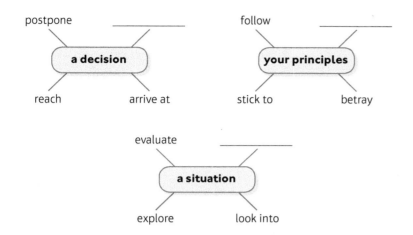

postpone _____   follow _____

a decision   **your principles**

reach   arrive at   stick to   betray

evaluate _____

a situation

explore   look into

B Each word web has two pairs of words with similar meanings. Draw a line to connect each pair.

C Match two collocations from Exercise 2B to each definition.
1 choose to do one thing or another   *arrive at a decision,*
2 delay deciding
3 be faithful to what you believe is right
4 do something that you don't believe is right
5 look at a situation in detail
6 judge a situation

3 A Read the extracts from a web forum below. Complete the texts with the correct form of the verbs from Exercise 2A. More than one answer is possible.

☆ At the store my food came to $10. I gave the cashier $20 but she gave me $100 in change. Obviously, she thought she'd given me a $10 note. I ¹_____ the situation – I needed money badly, it was her mistake. Should I ²_____ my principles and keep the money although I knew she might have to pay the missing cash back herself? In the end, I ³_____ a decision ...

☆ The night before my final school exams, a classmate sent me an email with the exam answers in an attachment. What should I do? Ignore the email or ⁴_____ the situation by asking him why he'd sent it and who else he'd sent it to? I really wanted to ⁵_____ my principles and do the exam without cheating. I ⁶_____ the decision by going to bed. In the morning, it was clear to me what to do ...

B Work in pairs and discuss.
1 What do you think each person did? Do you think that was a good decision?
2 Can you remember a time when you took a long time to reach a decision or where you decided to stick to your principles?

GRAMMAR

PAST AND MIXED CONDITIONALS

4 A Look at the sentences and underline all the verbs.
1 I think if any of us had used it, it would have felt really wrong.
2 If that had happened to me, I might not have jumped.
3 I would have done the same thing.
4 If he hadn't jumped down there, the baby wouldn't be alive.

B Work in pairs and answer the questions about sentences 1–4 above.
1 Do they refer to real or hypothetical situations?
2 Does each sentence refer to the past, or to the past and present?
3 Sentence 3 has only one (result) clause. Why is it unnecessary to have a conditional clause? In the second text find another example of a result clause on its own.

C Complete the rules with the words in the box.

modal (x2)   past perfect   *have*
infinitive   past participle

RULES

1 In the conditional clause use: the _____ to talk about the hypothetical past.
2 In the result clause use:
a) _____ + _____ + _____ to talk about the past.
b) _____ + _____ to talk about the present.

5 ▶ 8.1   **CONNECTED SPEECH: weak forms** Listen and match the words in bold in sentences 1–4 with the weak forms a)–d). Then listen again and repeat.
1 I **would have** done the same.
2 I **might have** behaved differently.
3 I **wouldn't have** been so brave.
4 I **couldn't have** done what he did.

a) /ˈmaɪtəv/
b) /ˈkʊdəntəv/
c) /ˈwʊdəntəv/
d) /ˈwʊdəv/

▷ page 132 **LANGUAGE BANK**

6 Read the situations 1–3 and complete the sentences a) and b) with the correct form of the verbs in brackets.

1 A hiker saved two strangers lost on a snowy mountain by sharing his food and water with them and risking his own life.

a) If they _____ (be) more prepared when they set out that morning, he _____ (not need) to risk his own life.

b) They _____ (be) dead now if he _____ (leave) them there.

2 A 39-year-old man saved a woman by pulling her out of her burning car, which exploded moments later.

a) They both _____ (could die) if it _____ (take) any longer to pull her out.

b) Most of the other people there _____ (not do) that.

3 A woman found a winning lottery ticket and used the money to buy a house. Later she had to return the money to the original owner of the ticket, who still had the receipt proving he had bought it.

a) I _____ (feel) pretty bad if I _____ (do) what that woman did, and if I'd been caught.

b) If the man _____ (not save) the receipt, he _____ (might never recover) the money.

SPEAKING

7 A Think of decisions you've made: good and bad, easy and hard, major and minor. Look at the topics for ideas, and make notes about two situations.

a subject you chose to study at school

a job you accepted or turned down

a trip you took, or almost took

an activity you took part in or avoided

a relationship you got into, or out of

a school or university you chose to attend

B Work with other students and take turns. Ask and answer questions 1–5 about each situation. Who had the most difficult decision?

1 Where did it happen?

2 What happened leading up to the situation?

3 How did you feel, and what did you do?

4 What else could you have done?

5 Would you do the same again?

VOCABULARY *PLUS*

COMPOUND ADJECTIVES

8 A Work in pairs and discuss. How could you reword these phrases without using the compound adjectives?

1 the 91-year-old widow

2 $4,000 in bubble-wrapped bills

3 bank-robbing daughter

B Work in pairs and find a compound adjective above which is formed with:

1 a past participle

2 a present participle (verb + -ing)

3 a number and measure of age/time

speakout TIP

Compound adjectives are made up of two or more words that form a single idea. They often have hyphens. With phrases expressing quantity, do not use a plural: *nine-month-old baby* NOT ~~nine-months-old baby~~.

C Complete the sentences using a compound adjective formed from the underlined words.

1 The baby is three days old. She's a …

2 I like clothes that people make by hand. I like …

3 That wall is 15 metres high. It's a …

4 That moment changed my life. It was a …

5 The TV series has run for a long time. It's a …

6 The course is five years long. It's a …

7 Elaine Jones has very good qualifications. She's very …

8 Research is an activity that consumes a lot of time. It's a …

9 A Rewrite the sentences using a compound adjective that expresses the meaning in brackets.

1 A _____ child shouldn't be left alone at home. (one who is twelve years old)

2 All outdoor cafés should be _____. (you can't smoke there)

3 A _____ holiday is too long. (it lasts two months)

4 It's hard for me to remember names, especially _____ names. (ones that sound odd)

5 Auto manufacturers should spend more money developing a _____ car. (solar energy powers it)

6 I would never live at the top of a _____ building. (it's twenty storeys)

B Tick (✓) the statements you agree with, and put a cross (✗) if you disagree. Then discuss with a partner.

▷ page 140 **VOCABULARYBANK**

FAIR SHARE

 G -ing form and infinitive
P connected speech: intrusive /w/
V values

((**8.2**

The Ultimatum Game

You have been given £10.
You have to offer some of
this money to your partner.
If your partner accepts your offer,
you split the money as agreed.
· If your partner rejects the offer,
neither of you keep anything.
You must decide how much
money to offer to your partner.

THE SHARING EXPERIMENT

The Dictator Game

You have been given £10.
You have to offer some of
this money to your partner.
Your partner has no choice
and has to accept your offer.
You must decide how much
money to offer to your partner.

SPEAKING

1 A Work in pairs and discuss. Read the instructions above for The Sharing Experiment, two games that test people's behaviour. What do you think the games show about people?

B Work alone. Imagine you are playing the games. Write an amount from £0–£10.

1 The Ultimatum Game:
I would keep £_____ and offer my partner £_____. The lowest I would accept from my partner is £_____.

2 The Dictator Game:
I would keep £_____ and offer my partner £_____.

C Compare your ideas with other students and discuss the questions.

1 How different are your results?
2 What did the two games show about your personality?
3 Do you think you would behave differently in a real-life situation than you did in the game?

VOCABULARY

VALUES

2 A Work in pairs. Match 1–6 with a)–f) to make sentences.

1 I think it shows that you have a sense of **fairness**, d
2 It brings out **aggression** in people. In fact,
3 I enjoyed being in **control**
4 Here there's no **equality** because
5 I imagine some people give more than they have to
6 There's no **justice** in this game,

a) just as there's none in real life. I felt cheated and hard done by.
b) and that's why I kept all the money for myself. I'm surprised at my own **greed.**
c) one person has less **power.**
d) especially if you split it 50-50 even though you don't have to.
e) and that sort of **generosity** always surprises me.
f) I think someone might try to hurt the other person.

B Write the words in bold in Exercise 2A next to their meanings.

1 being kind and willing to give
2 threatening behaviour
3 a situation where people have the same rights
4 the ability to make someone do something (2 words)
5 being reasonable in judgement (2 words)
6 strong desire for more money, food or other things

C Discuss in pairs. Does each sentence in Exercise 2A refer to the Ultimatum Game, the Dictator Game or both?

LISTENING

3 A ▶ 8.2 Listen to two people, Heather and Dominic, play the Ultimatum Game and answer the questions.

1 How much did Dominic offer Heather?
2 Did she accept?
3 What reasons does Dominic give for his decision?
4 What does Heather say about the decision?
5 What was the lowest amount Heather would have accepted?

B Discuss in pairs. Did anything surprise you about the outcome of the game? How do you think Heather and Dominic will behave in the Dictator Game?

C ▶ 8.3 Listen to them play the Dictator Game and answer the questions.

1 How much did Dominic offer Heather?
2 What reasons does he give for his decision?
3 What does Heather say about the decision?

D Work in groups and discuss.

1 How different were Dominic and Heather's results from yours in Exercise 1B?
2 How much do you identify with the reasons Dominic gave for his decisions in either game?
3 How much do you identify with Heather's reaction? Were your reactions very different?

GRAMMAR

-ING FORM AND INFINITIVE

4 A Check what you know. Complete the article using the correct form of the verb in brackets. Use the -ing form, the infinitive or the infinitive + to.

AN EXPERT COMMENTS ON
▶ **The Ultimatum Game**

Research shows that people tend ¹ _to respond_ (respond) differently depending on their cultural context and other factors. In Japan, players offered twice as much as those in Peru. But don't make the mistake of ² _____ (think) that Japanese are more generous than Peruvians. Perhaps ³ _____ (be) generous in the game means you want people ⁴ _____ (think) you are in real life. The game gives you the chance ⁵ _____ (act) unselfishly or not; some people are playing ⁶ _____ (impress) people. If it's important to someone ⁷ _____ (see) as fair, it's easy ⁸ _____ (act) that way in the game because it's just a game.

The Dictator Game is very interesting because no one would imagine a genuine dictator really ⁹ _____ (share) money. True, some players would ¹⁰ _____ (keep) everything, but most people let their partner ¹¹ _____ (have) a share of the money. Interestingly, most five-year-olds will ¹² _____ (share) at least half of the money – they're not interested in ¹³ _____ (have) the most. My opinion is that deep down most human beings would rather ¹⁴ _____ (cooperate) and avoid ¹⁵ _____ (exploit) others, in the game and in real life.

B Work in pairs and discuss. What surprised you the most? Do you agree with the last sentence?

C Work in pairs. Look at the verb forms 1–15 in the article and complete the table.

	-ing form, infinitive or infinitive + to	example
after a preposition		
to express purpose		
after *let someone* or *make someone*		
as part of a semi-fixed phrase, e.g. *It's important/ easy* and *the chance*		
as a subject or object (or part of one of these)		
after modal verbs		
after certain verbs, e.g. *enjoy, avoid, imagine*		
after certain verbs, e.g. *want, would like, tend*	*infinitive + to*	1
after *had better, would rather*		

▷ page 132 **LANGUAGEBANK**

5 A ▶ 8.4 Work in pairs. Complete each sentence with an alternative that means the same as the modal verb in brackets. Then listen and check.

1 I don't want _to have to_ refuse. (must)
2 I hate _____ argue to get my way. (must)
3 I don't seem _____ to stand up for myself. (can)
4 I enjoy _____ offer people help. (can)

B CONNECTED SPEECH: intrusive /w/ Work in pairs. In sentences 1–4, circle *to* where it is pronounced /tə/ and draw a box around it where it is pronounced /tuːw/.

C Listen again and check. What is the rule? Then listen and repeat.

6 A Cross out the incorrect forms in the sentences.

1 I would rather *being/to be/be* a victim of unfairness than an unfair person.
2 It's good that some parents make their children *working/to work/work* from an early age.
3 Everyone is capable of *cheating/ to cheat/cheat* another person, given the right circumstances.
4 Beware of anyone who says they can't stand *losing/to lose/lose*, as they'll do anything to win.
5 A child should *being/to be/be* taught when and how to be generous …
6 … but not just *earning/to earn/earn* the praise of others.
7 It's better *giving/to give/give* than *receiving/to receive/receive*.
8 *Being/To be/Be* good is easy; what is difficult is *being/to be/be* just. (Victor Hugo)

B Look at the sentences above. Tick (✓) two that you agree with, and put a cross (✗) next to two you disagree with.

C Work in groups and compare your ideas. Who in your group agreed with you the most?

speakout TIP

Record patterns after verbs and phrases, e.g. *would rather (do)*, and write an example: *I'd rather stay at home.* How might you record these phrases: *look forward to …, had better …* ?

WRITING

AN INFORMAL ARTICLE; LEARN TO USE LINKERS OF PURPOSE

7 A Read the article and choose the best title.
   a) Learn to be aggressive
   b) Life isn't fair
   c) Change the things you can

Do you hate it when people treat you unfairly? If you get a lower grade than you deserve, or you miss out on a promotion, do you lie awake all night fuming? Well, here are some things you can do about it to help you get past all that negativity.

First of all, it's important to remember that **for** a positive outcome, you need to maintain a positive attitude. It's much more difficult to change something if you're feeling angry or upset. If you know you're in the right, develop a can-do attitude **so as to** bring some positive energy to the situation.

Second, you have to get yourself to think rationally **so that** it's your head not your heart that dictates what you do. Don't get emotional **because** that'll only result in you making the situation worse; I've often made that mistake and lived to regret it. If you want to stand up for yourself or for someone else, you need to stay calm. That's how I managed to get a promotion recently after a long fight for justice.

Finally, you need to recognise the difference between things you can do something about, and things you can't. For example, once someone bumped into my car and drove away, and I couldn't really do anything about it; I had to accept the situation **in order to** move on. If on the other hand you see someone being unkind to someone else, you can say something to the person **to** change their behaviour as long as you do it clearly, firmly and unemotionally. They may not respond exactly as you'd like, but you'll have a better chance of influencing them.

With these ideas in mind, you can become much better at dealing with unfairness, and you might even have a positive influence on situations as well as people.

B Underline the correct alternative and give a reason.
   1 The article is probably for a *student magazine/ serious newspaper*.
   2 The aim of the article is to *describe/give advice*.
   3 The topic sentence is at the *beginning/end* of each main paragraph.

C Work in pairs and read the guidelines. Are they true (T) or false (F)? Find examples in the article.

In an informal article you should:
   1 give personal examples.
   2 use the pronouns *I* and *you*.
   3 avoid contracted forms.
   4 use conversational language.
   5 use linkers to help structure the article.
   6 use questions to the reader.
   7 avoid multi-word verbs.
   8 use the passive where possible.

8 A Work in pairs. Look at the linkers of purpose in bold in the article and answer the questions.
   1 Which linkers are followed by:
      a) an infinitive? *so as to (bring)*
      b) a subject + verb?
      c) a noun?
   2 Which two linkers can also be used in more formal situations?
   3 How do you change the following underlined linkers to make the sentences negative?
   Count to ten <u>in order to</u> lose your temper.
   Control your emotions <u>so as to</u> act with aggression.

B Rewrite the sentences replacing the underlined linkers with the ones in brackets.
   1 A good leader treats everyone equally <u>in order to</u> make everyone feel valued. (so that)
   2 When I'm upset I usually phone my sister <u>to</u> chat. (for)
   3 It's important to check everyone in a team reaches a decision together, <u>because</u> if you don't, someone will be left behind. (so as not to)
   4 In a good relationship, it's important to sit down together from time to time <u>so that</u> you make sure everything is OK. (to)
   5 Never make a decision late at night. Sleep on it <u>to</u> let your brain continue working overnight and you'll wake up knowing what to do. (because)
   6 In a family, it's good to have a list of tasks for each person, <u>because</u> then no one is given the feeling they are doing more than their fair share. (in order not to)

9 A Work in pairs and brainstorm a list of main ideas for an article about one or two of the following topics:
   • how to control your temper
   • how to make decisions
   • how to work as a team or a family
   • how to have a good marriage or relationship
   • how to do something that you know a lot about
   • how to be a good leader or teacher

B Choose the topic you like and discuss ideas for opening/closing paragraphs. Then write the article (250–300 words).

8.3))) HAVE YOU GOT A MINUTE?

F handling an awkward situation
P sentence stress and intonation
V behaviour

VOCABULARY

BEHAVIOUR

1 A Look at the pairs of adjectives. Are they similar (S) or different (D) in meaning? Use a dictionary to check.

1 supportive – unhelpful
2 diplomatic – tactful
3 sensitive – sensible
4 confrontational – collaborative
5 aggressive – assertive
6 direct – focused

B Which adjectives in Exercise 1A become opposites by adding/removing a prefix/suffix?

*supportive – **un**supportive*

C Work in pairs. Which adjectives above describe your manner when:

• you break bad news to someone?
• a friend is down or in trouble?
• making a complaint?
• you work on a project with someone?
• you are driving or cycling?
• trying to sort out a problem between two friends?

I think I'm tactful but also quite direct if I have to break bad news to someone.

▷ page 140 **VOCABULARYBANK**

FUNCTION

HANDLING AN AWKWARD SITUATION

2 A Work in pairs. Look at situations 1–3 and photos A–C. What would be the best way to handle each situation?

1 Your colleague has loud, personal conversations on the phone when you're trying to work.
2 A flatmate of yours keeps borrowing money and never pays you back.
3 You're the manager of an elegant restaurant and a waitress has come in with purple hair.

B Work in pairs. Read the tips and discuss.

🔍 |Search

Tips for talking things through

Sometimes we have to raise topics with someone which we find embarrassing or awkward. Following these five tips will help smooth the process and minimise hurt feelings.

1 Say clearly why you want to talk to them at the start.
2 Give the message clearly. Be specific.
3 Don't tell them what other people say or think.
4 Give them space to say what they think and feel.
5 Suggest a solution (if they don't).

---

3 A ▶ 8.5 Listen to the conversation. Are the statements true (T) or false (F)? Correct the false statements.

1 Liz owes Jim a small amount of money.
2 She wants to pay him back immediately.
3 She doesn't always keep her promises.
4 Jim wants her to pay a set amount of money each week.

B Listen again. Tick the tips in Exercise 2B that the man follows.

4 A Complete phrases 1–5. Then look at the audio script on pages 150–151 and check.

Preparing the listener
There's something I've been ¹_____ to talk to you about.

Giving the message
It's ²_____ that …
I hope you don't ³_____ this the wrong way, but …
I don't want you to get the wrong idea, but …

Getting the other person's point of view
Do you know ⁴_____ I mean?
Do you see where I'm coming from?
How does that ⁵_____?

B ▶ 8.6 **SENTENCE STRESS AND INTONATION**
Listen and underline the stresses in the phrases. Does the voice rise or fall at the end of each phrase? Why?

1 There's something I've been meaning to talk to you about.
2 I hope you don't take this the wrong way, but …
3 I don't want you to get the wrong idea, but …

C Listen again and repeat.

▷ page 132 **LANGUAGEBANK**

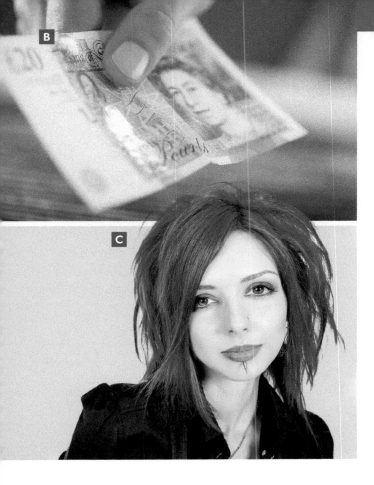

LEARN TO

SOFTEN A MESSAGE

6 A Work in pairs. Read the sentences below. When speaking, how could you soften the messages? What extra words or sounds could you add?

1 It's not that. I hope you don't take this the wrong way, but it's just that this isn't the first time I've lent you money and you haven't paid it back. I know it's not a lot, just small amounts each time, but it adds up quickly. I don't know. Do you know what I mean?

2 Actually, you've said that once before. I don't want you to get the wrong idea, but it never happened. And it makes things awkward. It makes me feel annoyed. Do you see where I'm coming from?

B ▶ **8.7** Listen to the sentences and add the extra words or sounds you hear.

speakout TIP

Fillers can help you sound less confrontational and allow thinking time. Some fillers (e.g. *um, er, well, you know, I mean, kind of*), are used instead of a pause. Modifiers (e.g. *just, a bit, slightly, quite*) often go before an adjective and soften a strong message (e.g. *I'm just a bit concerned = I'm VERY concerned*).

5 Work in pairs and role-play the situation. Use the flow chart to help.

Student A

there / something / I / mean / talk / you / about.

Student B

Yeah. What / up?

Well, look / don't / get / wrong idea, but …

But what?

It / just / I / very busy / you / always / phone.

Oh, right.

It / quite / annoying. / know / I / mean?

sorry / I / not / thinking.

I / suggestion. / Why / you / not / ask friends / call your mobile / instead of / land line?

You / mean / I / use / phone / different room?

That / right. / How / sound?

seem / reasonable. / really / sorry.

No problem. / Forget.

SPEAKING

7 A Work in pairs. For each situation below, write the first two sentences of the conversation.

1 You've been driving your colleague to work for over a month. He/She has never offered you money for petrol.

2 Your neighbour in a block of flats leaves bags of rubbish in the hall for days. He/She eventually takes them out but there's always a bad smell in the hall as a result.

3 Your friend has long conversations on her mobile when you're out together.

4 A friend often gives you a lift on his/her motorbike but his/her driving is scary.

B Role-play one of the situations.

C Work with another student and role-play a different situation.

8 Work with other students. Decide on the three most annoying things people do a) in your place of study or workplace b) at home.

DVD PREVIEW

1 A Work in pairs. Which gestures do you know? Show your partner.

1 shrug your shoulders
2 cross your fingers
3 tap the side of your head
4 give the thumbs up sign
5 hold your hands out, palms up
6 nod
7 shake your head
8 rub your thumb and first two fingers together

B What do these gestures mean in your country? Do people there use any other gestures?

2 Read the programme information and correct the sentences.

1 Desmond Morris observed human behaviour even though he's a bird-watcher.
2 He created a classification system for words people use with animals.
3 His project took him over sixty years and he travelled to many countries to complete it.
4 The programme looks at sign language.

◉)) The Human Animal

BBC

Desmond Morris is widely known for his study of human behaviour, customs and rituals, a 'man-watcher' in the same way as some people are bird-watchers. Originally a zoologist, Morris decided to observe and classify human behaviour in much the same way as he would observe animals – in his words 'to do for actions what dictionary makers had done for words.' His project of cataloguing human gesticulation and movement took him to over 60 countries and engrossed him for many years. In this programme in the series, Morris focuses on fascinating customs connected with greeting and on the meaning of different gestures.

DVD VIEW

3 A Before watching, discuss:

1 How many ways of shaking hands do you know?
2 How do you say 'You're crazy!' with your hands?

B Watch the DVD. Does Morris mention or show any of the things you talked about in Exercise 3A? Which handshake and 'You're crazy!' sign did you find the most interesting?

C Match the types of gesture to the countries. Then watch the DVD again and check.

Shaking hands:
1 Masai elders   a) shake and kiss hands
2 Mali, West Africa   b) continue until a deal is struck
3 Morocco   c) briefly touch the forearm
4 Kurdish farmers   d) give a quick palm touch

Saying 'You're crazy!':
1 Rome   a) twist finger round and round
2 England   b) circle finger anticlockwise
3 Japan   c) put fingers together and tap forehead
     d) tap side of head with finger

D Watch the DVD again and underline the correct alternative.

1 I *drew/directed* his attention to the fact that over the other side of the road there were two men who were *gesturing/gesticulating* in a particular way.
2 … a major new project, one that was to *keep my interest/engross me* for many years to come …
3 I began making huge charts naming every facial *gesture/expression*, every gesticulation, every movement, every *position/posture*.
4 Even the simplest human action such as the handshake has countless *differences/variations*.
5 The essential feature of handshaking is that it's an *equal/egalitarian* act.
6 They're all *exactly right for/fine-tuned to* the precise *context/situation* in which they occur.

speakout advice for a visitor

4 A ▶ 8.8 Listen to some advice for visitors to the USA. Is there anything that surprised you?

B Listen again and tick the key phrases that you hear.

> **KEY PHRASES**
>
> When people meet, they tend to …
> It's considered [good/bad] manners to …
> If you're not used to it, it can seem strange at first.
> It's not uncommon for people to …
> Having said that, don't be surprised if …
> It's [unacceptable/perfectly acceptable] to …

C Work in pairs or groups. Choose a country both of you know and prepare advice for visitors.

- Choose from the topics below and make notes on Do's and Don'ts for visitors.
- For each point, say why it is important and what can go wrong if a person doesn't know about the particular behaviour.

| Going out with friends – who pays? | Time keeping |

| Personal space, eye contact, posture, voice | Using names (first? last? title, e.g. *Mr*?) |

| Greetings | Paying/tipping in a restaurant |

| Special gestures | Saying goodbye |

| Going to someone's house for a meal |

D Present your information to other students. When you listen to other students, make notes of anything you didn't know before.

writeback cross-cultural article

5 A Read the short article giving advice on an aspect of behaviour in Britain. Which topics in Exercise 4C does it mention?

B Which things are the same as in your country?

Body language in Britain:
Keep your distance

British people are friendly, but there are some important things every visitor should know when spending time with them.

When you meet someone for the first time, it's normal to shake hands firmly, regardless of gender, both in formal and semi-formal situations. On subsequent meetings, this is not usually expected unless you haven't seen someone for a while. While the habit of exchanging kisses is a growing trend amongst younger people, it should not be initiated by visitors and should generally be restricted to family members and to people you have already met and like.

In terms of personal space, British people feel uncomfortable if you stand too close, so try to keep some distance. Also it's important to make eye contact when talking to Brits, but don't overdo it, or you'll come across as rude or impolite. Gestures such as hugging and backslapping are not recommended. On the whole, British people tend to be less demonstrative than some other nationalities. They do not raise their voices or use gestures a lot to emphasise a point and shouting is never acceptable.

If you keep these points in mind, you'll have a much more comfortable, enjoyable visit to Britain.

C Write a short article (150–200 words) giving advice to a foreign student or business person coming to your country. Choose one or two topics from Exercise 4C to focus on.

D Read other students' articles. What information do you find that you didn't know before?

ⓥ COLLOCATIONS

1 Underline the correct alternative in each sentence.

1 I had no time to *evaluate/stick to* the situation and had to act quickly – it was too dangerous to *postpone/reach* the decision till later.

2 I always try to *betray/stick to* my principles and never *go against/arrive at* them.

3 You should *explore/follow* the situation thoroughly and not be afraid of *doing/putting off* the decision.

4 We would like to take more time to *betray/assess* the situation before we *arrive at/follow* a final decision.

ⓖ PAST AND MIXED CONDITIONALS

2 A Underline the correct alternative in each sentence.

1 If I hadn't started studying English,
 a) I *might study/might have studied* another language.
 b) I *wouldn't go/wouldn't have gone* to university.
 c) I *wouldn't be/wasn't* able to watch films in English.

2 If I'd had the chance to live in a different country,
 a) I *wouldn't take/would have taken* it.
 b) I *would find/would have found* it very hard to make a decision about where.
 c) I *would choose/would have chosen* to live in Spain.

3 If computers hadn't been invented,
 a) the world *would be/had been* a less open place.
 b) people would *spend/have spent* more time together now.
 c) my parents would *end up/have ended up* in different jobs.

B For each sentence, circle the ending a), b) or c) that is most true for you.

C Work in pairs and compare your ideas.

ⓥ VALUES

3 A Add the vowels to complete the questions about values.

1 Is it possible to have f_ _rn_ss without _q_ _l_ty? How about when a disadvantaged person is given special treatment?

2 If kids play team sports, are they more likely to learn cooperation or _ggr_ss_ _n?

3 How can g_n_r_s_ty be used as a way of gaining c_ntr_l over people or a situation?

4 If you were a judge with total p_w_r, would you be able to practise perfect j_st_c_, and never show favour towards anyone – even family and friends?

5 You can press a button and eliminate either gr_ _d or ignorance from the face of the earth. Which one would it be?

B Work in pairs and ask and answer the questions.

ⓖ -ING FORM AND INFINITIVE

4 A Complete the sentences with the correct form of the words in brackets.

1 The most difficult thing about my day is _____ to and from work. (travel)

2 I've always been able _____ new words just by _____ them. (learn, hear)

3 It's not very good for a person _____ alone when they're depressed. (be)

4 I never have time _____ the things I really want to do. (do)

5 _____ a bike is one of my favourite ways of relaxing. (ride)

6 I study English for an hour a day but I keep _____ the same mistakes! (make)

7 I enjoy _____ films in English. (able / watch)

8 _____ a uniform is the worst part of my job. (have / wear)

B Tick any sentences you agree with. Make the others true for you.

C Work in pairs and take turns. Student A: read one of your sentences. Student B: ask follow-up questions.
A: The worst part of my job is …
B: Oh, why is that?

ⓕ HANDLING AN AWKWARD SITUATION

5 A Correct the mistake and add the missing word in each sentence.

1 Excuse me, Wendy. Do/have a ~~monument~~? *[you]* *moment*

2 There's nothing I've meaning to talk to you about.

3 Look, I want you to get the right idea, but …

4 It that just I've noticed that …

5 I feel brighter if …

6 How you fill about that?

B Work in pairs. Choose one of the situations below and practise the conversation. Student A: use all of the sentences from Exercise 5A in order. Then choose another situation and exchange roles with Student B.

• telling a colleague that their clothing isn't appropriate for the workplace
• telling a friend that they always forget your birthday and it bothers you
• telling a student they didn't pass an important exam

Excuse me, Juan. Do you have a moment? There's something I've been meaning to talk to you about …

9) trouble

WITNESS p104

SCAM p107

IT'S AN EMERGENCY! p110

SURVIVAL p112

BBC INTERVIEWS

◉)) Do you have any phobias?

103

9.1))) WITNESS

G -ing form and infinitive
P connected speech: elision
V crime; dependent prepositions

VOCABULARY

CRIME

1 A Work in pairs and discuss. What crimes are the most common in your city/town?

B Work in pairs and complete the newspaper extracts with the crimes in the box.

> kidnapping hacking stalking vandalism
> identity theft bribery counterfeiting mugging
> arson shoplifting

1 A teenager has been accused of _____ after he was seen setting fire to an empty factory.

2 He was jailed for five years for _____ into government computer systems.

3 There has been a reduction in _____ in stores after the introduction of more security guards.

4 A man has been found guilty of _____ film star Halle Berry. He followed her everywhere.

5 There have been several cases of _____ of foreign journalists. In the latest case, a demand was made for $500,000.

6 _____ is a problem, with officials accepting money from companies that want to do business in the country.

7 There were no witnesses to the act of _____ in which a statue was damaged.

8 Police arrested three people for _____ dollars. More than a million fake $50 bills were found.

9 Banks revealed that cases of _____ have doubled. Customers are warned to keep PIN numbers more secure.

10 The increase in CCTV cameras has cut cases of late-night _____ in town centres.

C Complete the table for the words in Exercise 1B. Use your dictionary to help if necessary. Add any other crime vocabulary you know.

crime	person	verb
arson	arsonist	to commit arson
hacking		

D Work with other students and discuss.

1 Which ones do you think are the most serious crimes and which are more minor offences?

2 Are any of the crimes serious problems in your country?

3 Do you know anyone who has had experience of any of these crimes?

Memories **on trial**

Even in these days of DNA tests and other forensic techniques, witness testimony still plays an important part in court cases. But how reliable are our memories? BBC *Focus* magazine's Andy Ridgway finds we know less than we think ...

READING

2 A Work in pairs and discuss. Do you have a good memory? What do you remember easily? What do you have difficulty remembering?

B Read the article and find two examples of false memories.

C Read the article again. Are statements 1–6 true (T) or false (F)? Underline any words/phrases that help you decide.

1 In court, evidence from a witness is not important if there are other kinds of evidence.

2 Forty percent of people in one study were able to give a full description of the film of the bus exploding in Tavistock Square.

3 A poor memory doesn't usually matter in day-to-day life, according to the article.

4 In 1998, in the USA, almost all major criminal cases depended entirely on witness evidence.

5 The rumour about the white van was started by one witness.

6 One in five witnesses makes a mistake in ID parades.

D Look at the article again. What do the six highlighted words refer to? Draw an arrow backwards or forwards to the word/phrase.

Most of us have some recollection of the 2005 terrorist attacks in London. It could well be a mental image of ...

E Work in pairs and discuss. Who/What does the author blame for false convictions? Would you make a good witness?

> In ID parades, forty percent of witnesses identified the police's suspect.
> In forty percent of cases no identification was made.
> In twenty percent of cases they pointed to a volunteer.

Most of us have some recollection of the 2005 terrorist attacks in London. It could well be a mental image of a red double-decker bus in Tavistock Square with its roof ripped off by the force of the explosion. That's not surprising given the number of photographs of the damaged bus that were carried in newspapers in the days after the attack.

But what about CCTV footage? Do you remember seeing a video of the bus exploding? What can you see in that video?

Well, the truth is, you shouldn't be able to see anything in your mind's eye because such CCTV footage simply doesn't exist. But don't worry. If it only took a suggestion that you may have seen a video of the explosion to create an image in your mind, you're not alone. In fact, in a study carried out by Dr James Ost at the University of Portsmouth, forty percent of people claimed to have seen this nonexistent footage. Some even went on to describe what happened in vivid detail.

Many of us think we have a good memory. After all, it's got us through the occasional exam. But what Ost's study clearly demonstrates is just how easily influenced our memories are. 'Facts' from the past can become confused in our minds. And it can simply be the fact that we've been asked about something, such as a nonexistent video clip, that can alter our memory.

In many cases, an unreliable memory is not a problem. It just means we forget to send a birthday card on time or a story we tell at a party is not one hundred percent accurate. But sometimes the contents of our memories can have huge consequences – putting people behind bars or even, in the USA, on Death Row.

In 1998, an American study calculated that in ninety-five percent of felony cases – the more serious crimes – witness evidence (in other words, people's memories) was the only evidence heard in court. In the UK, despite DNA and other forensic evidence being used more regularly, witness memories are still a vital part of court proceedings.

Even before a case gets to court, a few false memories can get an investigation off to a bad start. In the sniper attacks that took place in the Washington DC area in 2002, witnesses reported seeing a white van or truck fleeing several of the crime scenes. A white vehicle may have been seen near one of the first shootings and the media began repeating this. When they were caught, the sniper suspects were actually driving a blue car. It seems many witness memories had been altered by the media reports. ■

GRAMMAR

-ING FORM AND INFINITIVE

3 A Underline the correct alternative in sentences 1–3. Then check in the article.

1 Do you remember *to see/seeing* a video of the bus exploding?

2 Some even went on *to describe/describing* what happened in vivid detail.

3 It just means we forget *to send/sending* a birthday card on time.

B Work in pairs and check what you know. What is the difference in meaning between the pairs of phrases in bold?

1 a) I **remembered to set** the alarm before I left.
  b) I **remember thinking** the building was quiet.

2 a) I **forgot to buy** tickets for the Adele concert.
  b) I'll never **forget seeing** Adele in concert.

3 a) Henri **stopped to drink** some coffee.
  b) Then he **stopped driving** as he still felt tired.

4 a) After lengthy training, Billy **went on to become** a famous dancer.
  b) Billy **went on practising** every day even when he was famous.

5 a) He **tried to recall** her name, but couldn't.
  b) He **tried going** through the alphabet to remember it.

6 a) We **regret to inform** you that the concert has been cancelled.
  b) And I **regret spending** so much on the ticket!

C Match rules 1–12 below with meanings a) or b). Use the examples in Exercise 3B to help.

RULES		
1 remember doing	**a)** do something that is one's responsibility
2 remember to do	**b)** have a memory of something
3 forget doing **4** forget to do	**a)** not do something that is one's responsibility **b)** not have a memory of something
5 stop doing **6** stop to do	**a)** finish an action **b)** finish an action in order to do something else
7 go on doing **8** go on to do	**a)** do something after finishing something else **b)** continue an action
9 try doing **10** try to do	**a)** experiment with an activity **b)** make an effort to do something difficult
11 regret doing **12** regret to do	**a)** be sorry about something you are about to do **b)** be sorry about something you did in the past

4 ▶ **9.1** CONNECTED SPEECH: elision Listen and write the sentences. Cross out letters at word endings that are not pronounced. Then listen and repeat.

I remembered to lock up.

▷ page 134 **LANGUAGEBANK**

5 A Complete the questions with the correct form of the verbs in the box.

get study buy write hide take help become witness think inform do

1 If someone stole your wallet, would you run after them and try _to get_ it back?

2 Have you ever forgotten _____ a ticket for a train journey, then got caught?

3 If you were in a hurry and you saw an accident but there were lots of people around, would you stop _____?

4 Is there an event in your country you'll never forget _____, because it was so significant?

5 Is there anything thing you regret not _____ when you were a child?

6 Do you ever stay awake at night because you can't stop _____ about a problem?

7 Do you always remember _____ breaks when you're studying hard?

8 Has anyone you knew as a child gone on _____ famous?

9 Have you ever tried _____ on your hand as a way of reminding yourself to do something?

10 You open a letter that says, 'I regret _____ you that your application has been refused.' What's it referring to?

11 How long do you think you'll go on _____ English?

12 Do you sometimes remember _____ something 'in a safe place' but find you've forgotten where you put it?

B Work in pairs and ask and answer the questions.

SPEAKING

6 A Work alone. How would you have acted if you'd witnessed a crime? Read situations 1–4 and make notes on what you would have done. Use questions a)–c) to help you.

1 You caught a pickpocket trying to take your mobile and he threatened to hurt you if you called the police.

2 You saw a friend shoplifting in a department store.

3 You noticed a colleague stealing office supplies from your place of work.

4 You witnessed your neighbour's teenage children committing an act of vandalism, e.g. spraying graffiti on the wall of their school.

a) Would you have intervened or try to stop the person?

b) Would you have reported the person to the authorities?

c) If you'd been questioned by the authorities, would you have told the truth?

B Work in groups and compare your ideas.

VOCABULARY *PLUS*
DEPENDENT PREPOSITIONS

7 A Work in pairs. Complete the headlines with a preposition and the correct form of the verbs in brackets.

1 FAKE POLICE OFFICER CHARGED _____ £600 NECKLACE (steal)

2 Woman accuses con artist _____ bag and PIN (take)

3 Gang arrested _____ one car nine times (sell)

B Write the headlines in full. Which are active and which passive?

1 *A fake police officer has been charged with stealing a £600 necklace. passive*

C Complete the headlines using a dependent preposition and the correct form of the verbs in brackets. Then check with a partner or in a dictionary.

1 Hacker suspected _____ government computers (access)

2 Student apologises _____ in exam (cheat)

3 President blames 'greedy' banks _____ crisis (cause)

4 Local girl dreams _____ top talent (become)

5 Agency criticised _____ size-zero models (employ)

6 Train company bans teenager _____ for one year (travel)

7 Mother thanks toddler _____ her life (save)

8 Animal rights activists rescue lobster _____ (be eat)

9 Jury clears actress _____ husband number three (murder)

10 Dolphin saves swimmer _____ (drown)

8 A Work in pairs. Choose two of the headlines above and write a news article in three sentences.

B Work in groups and take turns. Student A: read out your article. Other students: close your book and say the appropriate headline.

▷ page 141 **VOCABULARYBANK**

SCAM

G past modals of deduction
P connected speech: past modals
V synonyms

((9.2

VOCABULARY

SYNONYMS

1 A Read the dictionary extract. Think of an example of a scam.

> **S** **scam** /skæm/ *n* [C] *informal* a clever but dishonest way to get money

From Longman Active Study Dictionary.

B Work in pairs. Read the infographic and answer the questions.

1 What are your answers to the first two questions in the text?

2 Which of the five scams can be done by one person?

C Match meanings 1–6 with two of the underlined verbs or verb phrases in the infographic. Write the verb phrases in the infinitive.

1 act as if you're someone else *pretend to be,*

2 trick someone

3 cause somebody to <u>not</u> notice something

4 take something quickly

5 believe a trick

6 exchange one thing for another

speakout TIP

Use synonyms to improve your speaking and writing. You can a) notice synonyms when you read b) record them in your notebook c) look up synonyms in a thesaurus or on the internet d) use synonyms when writing to avoid repetition.

Rewrite the following, using synonyms for *nice*: *Yesterday was very nice. I had a nice meal at a nice restaurant with some nice people.*

LISTENING

2 A ▶ 9.2 Listen to the conversations. Which two scams from the infographic happened to the people?

B Work in pairs and try to complete the statements. Then listen again and check your ideas.

1 The thieves distracted Lise by …

2 She trusted the man because …

3 She thought she was talking to the bank on the phone because …

4 The thieves got her PIN code by …

5 The man in the jewellery shop was posing as …

6 He accused the woman of …

7 He left the shop with …

8 Dan thought that the man was going to …

3 Work in pairs and discuss the questions.

1 What should/shouldn't the people have done in each situation?

2 Why do you think people fall for scams?

3 Have you read or heard about any other scams (over the phone, internet or face-to-face)?

Scam-proof yourself

How easily do you think you could <u>be taken in</u> by a professional con artist? Is it easy for a well-dressed but ill-intentioned stranger to <u>deceive</u> you and walk away with your money, credit cards or phone? Once you understand the basic principles of street scams, you'll never <u>fall for</u> a scam again.

1) The Shoulder Surf

You're standing at the ATM and some nice person asks if that's your 20 euros on the ground. An innocent question, or a trick to <u>distract</u> you so they can <u>snatch</u> your card out of the slot?

2) The Fake Police Officer

If a man walked into a shop where you worked and <u>pretended to be</u> a police officer, would he <u>fool</u> you?

3) Escalator Jam

As you reach the bottom of the escalator, suddenly there's a jam of people and you get bumped into. You drop your mobile, but a kind woman picks it up and gives it back to you. Are you sure she hasn't <u>switched</u> it for an identical (but broken) one?

4) The Tourist Photo

'Can you take our photo?' It's just one of many ways to <u>divert your attention</u> so the hustlers can easily <u>grab</u> your wallet or mobile or <u>swap</u> it for an identical one.

5) The Squirt

A stranger bumps into you and gets ketchup all over your jacket! How nice that some people are helping you wipe it off … or are they just thieves <u>posing as</u> helpful passersby?

GRAMMAR

PAST MODALS OF DEDUCTION

4 A Match sentences 1–7 with meanings a)–c).

1 It can't have been the young couple because I was looking at them all the time.
2 So it must have been stolen when I was taking the photo.
3 He must have taken my bag when I wasn't looking.
4 He could have hidden it in his case.
5 The woman must have been working with the guy.
6 She couldn't have been a real customer.
7 But she might have had fake money.

a) I'm almost certain this happened.
b) I feel it's possible this happened.
c) I'm almost certain this didn't happen.

B Complete the rules. Use the sentences in Exercise 4A to help.

RULES	1 To speculate or make a deduction about something that happened in the past, use the modals: *must /_____/_____/_____/_____ + have + _____.* 2 To emphasise that an activity was in progress, use modal + *have +* _____ + _____. 3 In the passive, use modal + *have +* _____ + _____.

5 A ▶ 9.3 **CONNECTED SPEECH: past modals** Listen to the pronunciation of the past modals in connected speech. Then listen again and repeat.

must have	could have	might have	can't have	couldn't have
/mʌstəv/	/kʊdəv/	/maɪtəv/	/kɑːntəv/	/kʊdəntəv/

B ▶ 9.4 Listen to the phrases and repeat.

must have, must have been, It must have been great!

▷ page 134 **LANGUAGEBANK**

6 A Complete the accounts of two scams. Use modals of deduction and the verbs in brackets.

I was taking out money at an ATM. Just as my card came out, a guy behind me said I'd dropped some money. Sure enough, there was a twenty-euro note on the floor. I bent down, picked it up and my card was gone … and so was the man! He ¹_____ (drop) the twenty-euro note and pretended it was mine, or the note ²_____ (fall) out of my wallet and he simply took advantage of the situation. He ³_____ (pull) my card out of the ATM when I bent down.

An estate agent was showing me a flat when she got a phone call from another customer who wanted to put down a deposit on that same flat. So I gave the agent my deposit, signed the contract, and was given the key. When I went back later to move in, the key didn't work … and the agent didn't answer her phone number! The woman ⁴_____ (be) an estate agent. She ⁵_____ (be) an imposter and the other customer ⁶_____ (work) with her.

B Discuss in pairs. Which scam in Exercise 6A would be most likely to fool you?

SPEAKING

7 A Work in pairs. Student A: turn to page 146. Student B: imagine the following situation happened to you. Add some details about the place, time, the amount of money spent on the gifts and your feelings. Prepare to tell Student A.

It was [name of a festival] and everyone was buying presents. I was in a shopping mall and I'd bought some games and a camera for people in my family. In the middle of the mall there was a big sign saying 'Free Gift Wrapping', so I left the presents with a woman there and collected them half an hour later. On the morning of [name of festival], the kids opened their presents and inside the boxes there were just oranges and straw.

B Tell Student A the situation and discuss these questions.

1 Who swapped the presents?
2 How did they trick people into giving them the presents?
3 Why didn't people notice that the presents felt different?
4 How do you think the scam was done?

C Now listen to Student A's situation and discuss his/her questions.

D Turn to page 144 to see if your ideas were right.

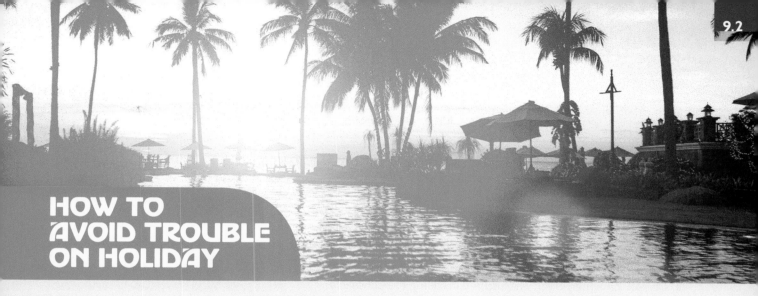

HOW TO AVOID TROUBLE ON HOLIDAY

Taxis

Be careful when taking taxis, especially at the airport. As an unsuspecting tourist, you may find yourself charged up to three times the normal fare or in a taxi with a driver who claims to have no change.

- Never **take** a taxi without a company name on its side.
- Always **ask** the approximate fare before getting in.
- **Phone** for a taxi ahead of time rather than catching one in the street.
- Make sure you **carry** plenty of change with you.

Money

Be careful around any major tourist sites. Pickpockets often work in gangs and will come up behind you while you're walking and unzip your backpack or may 'accidentally' bump into you and steal your money or mobile before passing these on immediately to a partner. Also, take care when using an ATM. A tiny hidden camera may have been installed to steal your card number and PIN.

- **Keep** your credit cards and larger sums of money in a money belt under your clothes.
- Be sure to **keep** any money that you think you'll use that day loose in your pocket, so that you don't need to pull out large notes.
- Be particularly careful to **cover** the keypad when you enter your PIN into an ATM machine.
- **Use** ATMs inside a bank where they are less likely to have been interfered with.

Tours

If someone offers a 'budget' tour, you may find that the price is cheap but you'll spend more time at shopping places not on your itinerary than the places you intended to visit. This is because your 'guide' is being paid by the shopkeepers for taking you there.

- **Book** tours only with reputable companies.
- Try to **check** with other visitors or with your hotel before booking a tour.
- Take time to **look** on the internet for reviews and recommendations.

WRITING

A 'HOW TO' LEAFLET; LEARN TO AVOID REPETITION

8 A Work in pairs. What advice would you give a visitor to a city about how to avoid getting into trouble?

B Read the extract from a 'how to' leaflet for tourists. Which ideas are different from the ones you discussed?

C Complete the guidelines for writing a 'how to' leaflet with the words in the box.

> bullet points   title   fonts   sections   contracted   subheading   underlining

1. Give the leaflet an overall _____.
2. Divide the leaflet into different _____, each with its own short _____.
3. Use different _____ or _____ so that it is easier for the reader to see the main points before they start reading.
4. Use _____ when you are writing a list.
5. To make your leaflet more direct and informal, use 'you' and _____ forms.

9 A Look at the verbs in bold in the leaflet and:

1. put a box around two adverbs used before the verbs.
2. underline five verb phrases used before the verbs.
3. circle the remaining four imperatives.

B Complete the rules and examples with words from the leaflet.

To avoid repetition when giving a list of advice:

1. use the adverbs ___*always*___ and _____.
2. use a range of synonyms (words/phrases) in the imperative:
   a) Make _____ you
   b) Be _____ to
   c) Be particularly _____ to
   d) Try _____
   e) Take _____ to

10 Write a 'how to' leaflet (200–250 words) on one of the following topics. Use a variety of ways to give advice and avoid repetition.

- advice for people travelling solo
- advice for internet banking
- advice for passing exams
- advice for joining a particular social networking site
- advice for (your own idea)

- **F** reporting an incident
- **P** sentence stress
- **V** incidents

SPEAKING

1 A Work in pairs and look at the photos. What would you do if you witnessed these situations?

B Work in pairs and discuss.

1 List three situations in which you think you should phone the emergency services.

2 Read the reasons for calling the emergency services below. Which reason do you think is the most ridiculous?

3 Do you think the person was justified in calling the police in any of the situations?

Police are becoming concerned because a significant percentage of calls to the emergency services are about everyday inconveniences and problems or are simply ridiculous. Some of the silliest calls include:

- I need help with my maths homework.
- I'm having a bad dream. In fact this is part of it.
- My husband's snoring and I can't sleep.
- There's a squirrel on my porch and it's acting suspiciously.
- The weather report was wrong. And now I'm stuck in the snow.
- I'm stuck in traffic and need to get to the toilet.
- My boyfriend promised to marry me and now he won't.
- I'm locked in a house. Not my house – I'm a burglar.

VOCABULARY

INCIDENTS

2 A Complete sentences 1–10 with the correct form of a verb phrase in the box.

fall off   get stuck   knock over   break down   lock out
run over   get knocked out   be on fire   steal   rob

1 'My card has _____ in the machine.'
2 'The house _____ – there's smoke coming from the windows.'
3 'We crashed into a lamp post and _____ it _____.'
4 'My car has _____ on the motorway.'
5 'My wallet has _____.'
6 'A workman on my roof has just _____ the ladder.'
7 'I've _____ myself _____ of my house.'
8 'I fell down but I don't remember anything after that. I think I _____.'
9 'Someone's just _____ my cat and I think they've killed it.'
10 'I've just _____! Someone's taken my bag from the changing room.'

B Work in pairs. Look at the sentences above and discuss.

1 Who might the person be phoning in each case?
2 What two questions might the other person ask the caller?
3 Which situations would you find the easiest to deal with?

1 In number one, they might be phoning the security department in a bank.

▷ page 141 **VOCABULARYBANK**

FUNCTION

REPORTING AN INCIDENT

3 A ▶ 9.5 Listen to the phone conversation. What happened to the man?

B Listen again and complete the report form.

INCIDENT REPORT 2047561A

Name: _____
Date and time of incident: _____
Location of incident: _____
Description of incident (what exactly happened?): _____
_____
Description of stolen or damaged property (serial number, bank card type, value of property, colour, make, model of car, etc.): _____
_____
Description of suspect or offender (age, sex, ethnicity, build, clothing, distinguishing marks or features, etc.):
_____
Witnesses: _____
Contact details: _____
_____

4 A ▶ 9.6 **Complete the phrases. Then listen and check.**

1 _____ I realised what _____ _____, he had run on.

2 It was _____ about thirty seconds _____ _____ I realised my wallet _____ _____.

3 But did it _____ your _____ that it wasn't just an accident?

4 It never _____ to me _____ he'd done it on purpose.

5 My mind just went _____.

6 He looked _____ _____ he was just out jogging.

7 It _____ _____ so quickly.

8 He just _____ _____ a normal guy.

9 He _____ me a bit _____ that actor.

10 I didn't _____ what he said. It was too quick.

B Work in pairs. Which phrases above a) describe impressions of a person b) refer to time?

C SENTENCE STRESS Underline the main stressed syllables in sentences 1–10 in Exercise 4A. Listen and check. Then listen and repeat.

Before I realised what had happened, he had run on.

▷ page 134 **LANGUAGEBANK**

5 Work in pairs and role-play the conversation between a police officer and a caller whose bag has been stolen from a shop changing room. Use the flow chart to help.

Police officer

Ask about the time and place.

Caller

Answer. Explain what happened.

Express surprise. (*Didn't it occur …*)

Answer. (*It crossed … It all happened …*)

Ask what they did.

Reply. (*As soon as I …*)

Ask if they saw anyone. Ask for a description.

Say 'yes'. Give a description. (*He/She reminded me …*)

Check the information.

Agree or correct the information.

6 Work in pairs.

Student A: choose a situation from Exercise 2A and phone the police to report what happened.

Student B: you are the police officer. Use the report form in Exercise 3B to ask questions.

LEARN TO

REPHRASE

7 A Look at the extract. Underline two places where the police officer (A) rephrases something to help the caller (B) understand.

A: Could you tell me exactly when the incident happened?

B: Just now. About an hour ago.

A: Could you be more precise?

B: Excuse me?

A: Could you give me the exact time?

B: I think at 2.50 or 2.55.

A: And where did it happen?

B: Park Avenue.

A: Can you pinpoint the exact location?

B: Pinpoint?

A: Tell me exactly where.

B Match the meaning of the words in bold in 1–5 with phrases a)–e) below.

1 I'll need **to take a statement**.

2 And he **hit into** me **hard** …

3 … **a sweater**, grey colour, **with a – you know – something you put over your head**.

4 … some sort of dark **trousers, for running or for the gym**.

5 And were there any other people **in the vicinity**?

a) in the surrounding area – nearby

b) tracksuit bottoms

c) a hood … a hoodie

d) to write down some details

e) collided with

C ▶ 9.7 Listen and check your answers.

speakout TIP

Using familiar words to explain unfamiliar vocabulary not only helps communication but can also be an opportunity to learn more sophisticated vocabulary.

SPEAKING

8 A Work in pairs. There was a burglary in your house last night. Student A: turn to page 146. Student B: turn to page 144.

B Work in pairs. Student B: ask Student A how the burglar got into the house. Draw a line showing his route. Help Student A with difficult vocabulary.

A: The burglar first climbed the … thing for rainwater … going down …

B: It's like a pipe, right? Which one?

A: Yes, like a pipe. The one on the left.

C Change roles. Student A: ask Student B how the burglar got out of the house. Draw a line showing his route. Help Student B with difficult vocabulary.

DVD PREVIEW

1 A Work in pairs and discuss.

1 What are different ways that people react in a disaster situation? Think about a building on fire, a sinking ship or a plane making a crash landing.

2 What do you think survival in a disaster depends on?

3 Which factors are connected to the character of the survivor?

B Read the programme information. What factors for survival does it mention? What do you think it means by 'how your brain reacts'?

 Horizon: How to survive a disaster **BBC**

When disaster strikes, who lives and who dies is not purely a matter of luck. In every disaster, from those people face once in a lifetime, to those they face every day, there are things that can be done to increase the chances of getting out alive. Some of these things have to do with planning ahead, some have to do with how your brain reacts, and some are simply down to luck. In this programme, we look at the sinking of the car ferry *Estonia* in 1994 through the experience of Paul Barney, a passenger on the *Estonia*, and examine why it is that he ended up among the survivors.

DVD VIEW

2 A Watch the DVD. Why did Paul Barney survive while others didn't?

B Are the statements true (T) or false (F)? Watch the DVD again and check your ideas.

1 Paul Barney slept in the cafeteria below the waterline.

2 He said he wasn't scared on board the ship, but was in the life raft.

3 One hundred and thirty-seven people died on the *Estonia*.

4 His tunnel vision caused him to focus on saving himself.

5 Professor Silke said that tunnel vision is not always a good thing.

6 Paul doesn't understand why some people didn't try to escape.

7 Most people keep a clear head in a disaster.

C Work in pairs. Complete the extracts by writing three words in each gap. Then watch the DVD again to check.

1 … I say to them really that there was no time _____, there was literally no time.

2 It was a very scary place to be because you never knew whether the next wave was going to _____ from the life raft.

3 I'm purely thinking of what's going to _____.

4 … our brain is focusing on whatever the threat or danger is, and it's focusing on that to the exclusion _____.

5 One of the things I remember clearly is the water actually coming into the cafeteria and seeing lots of people around just _____ spot.

D Work in pairs and discuss. How do you think you would react in a disaster like this? Would you be like Paul or would you be like one of the people he describes as 'rooted to the spot'?

speakout agreeing priorities

3 A ▶ 9.8 Listen to people deciding on things to take on a life raft. Which items below do they talk about? Why do they decide to take/reject each one?

- blankets
- tinned food
- torch (with generator)
- lighter
- dried fruit
- plastic raincoat
- first aid kit
- hand mirror
- fishing kit (line, hook)
- sun cream
- survival manual
- drinking cup

B Look at the key phrases. Listen again and tick the phrases you hear.

> **KEY PHRASES**
>
> It depends on [what/whether] …, doesn't it?
> It's important to … isn't it?
> It's (not) a top priority to be able to …
> What would we do with a … ?
> I'd say that … is/are [essential/vital/crucial]
> … to keep you [warm/dry/alive],
> … to [prevent/keep/protect] you from [the sun/dehydrating/getting …]
> [It/That] hadn't occurred to me.
> We need to prioritise them.
> I can't see the point of [taking, choosing] …

C Work alone and choose six items from the list in Exercise 3A. Make notes on why they are important and why other items are not as important.

D Work in groups and take turns. Try to persuade the other students that your choices are important then decide on six items as a group.

writeback an escape story

4 A A website has asked readers to write a story about a lucky escape prompted by a string of words. Work in pairs and discuss. What story can you imagine for the word string below?

> August   camping   forest   dry   tent
> sleep   smoke   fire   trapped   soup
> escape

B Read the story. What happened and how did the man get out of the situation without being hurt?

> It was mid-August, and some friends and I went camping in a forest about an hour's drive from where we were living. It had been a very dry summer and we should have thought about the dangers of fire, but we didn't. We pitched our tents, made a campfire and cooked a nice soup for dinner. After a while we were all quite tired, so we went to sleep.
>
> About an hour later I woke up to the smell of smoke. I realised straightaway that there was a fire, and that it was right in front of the tent – in fact some dry leaves next to the campfire had caught fire, and the front of the tent was starting to burn. I was trapped inside.
>
> Luckily, one of my friends who was in another tent woke up too, and he poured the leftover soup on the burning tent. That made it possible for me to escape, and I crawled out as fast as I could. We put out the campfire but I couldn't go back to sleep. I think I was in shock – it was a very lucky escape.

C Choose another word string. Write your story (150–250 words) using three paragraphs.

> spring   countryside   lost   dark   fence
> garden   dog   sandwich   run   jump   escape

> sea   cool   friends   swim   snorkel   hours
> tired   cold   stiff   drowning   save   escape

D Read other students' stories. Which one do you think was the most unusual escape?

Ⓥ CRIME

1 A Make a list of as many crimes as you can remember.

B Work in pairs and think of:

1 two crimes that involve damage to property.
2 three crimes that involve people and can happen on the street.
3 three crimes that involve technical expertise on computers or other machines.
4 a crime involving money that could be committed by a company.
5 a crime that involves theft but not usually in a street.

C Work in pairs and discuss. Which crimes are most often in the news in your town/city/country?

Ⓖ -*ING* FORM AND INFINITIVE

2 A Underline the correct alternatives in the article.

> → OK, you've just been mugged. Your first impulse may be to go on ¹*doing/to do* whatever you were doing, but don't. First, stop ²*checking/to check* that you're fine. Some victims who have been struck actually forget ³*being/to be* hit and only discover injuries later. Try ⁴*finding/to find* a safe place, maybe a café with people (you may need to borrow a phone). You're probably in shock – give yourself time to stop ⁵*shaking/to shake* and take slow, deep breaths to calm yourself. If this doesn't work, try ⁶*drinking/to drink* some cool water – avoid coffee. Remember ⁷*phoning/to phone* someone you know and tell them where you are and what happened. If you remember ⁸*seeing/to see* what the mugger looked like, write down the details. If you forget ⁹*doing/to do* this you may find that you can't recall much detail later when you talk to the police, and you'll regret not ¹⁰*doing/to do* this.

B Work in pairs and discuss. Which ideas do you agree with?

Ⓥ SYNONYMS

3 A Rewrite the sentences with a synonym for the words/phrases in bold.

1 Does listening to music when you study **divert your attention**?
2 Can you **snatch** fifteen minutes' sleep in the middle of the day?
3 Would you find it easier **to pretend to be** someone older or younger?
4 If you exaggerate your internet profile, are you **fooling** people unacceptably?
5 Have you ever **been taken in by** a lie someone told you?
6 Imagine you could **swap** identities with someone for just one day. Who would it be?

B Work in pairs and take turns. Ask and answer the questions.

Ⓖ PAST MODALS OF DEDUCTION

4 A Work in pairs and read the situations. For each one, rewrite the options using a modal of deduction.

1 A man checked his post box every day but it was always empty. Meanwhile his friends sent him dozens of letters a week.
   a) I'm sure the man moved recently. *The man must have moved recently.*
   b) Maybe his friends sent mail to the old address.
   c) I'm certain the postman didn't deliver the letters.
2 A pianist performed a concert in a concert hall. She played perfectly but at the end no one clapped.
   a) She was probably practising in an empty concert hall.
   b) I'm certain she was deaf.
   c) They definitely didn't like the music.

B Look at the extra information below and make a final guess to explain each situation. Then turn to page 146 and check your ideas.

1 The friends wrote the correct address on the letters. The postman always put the letters in the post box. There wasn't a hole in the bottom of the post box.
2 The concert hall was full. No one had hearing problems – everyone heard the performance and liked it.

Ⓕ REPORTING AN INCIDENT

5 A Complete the sentences with the correct form of a word in the box. One of the words is not used.

> ~~occur~~ if go not catch remind become like cross realise happen (x2)

1 It *occurred* to me that he/she shouldn't have …
2 He/She _____ me of …
3 It was only later that I _____ …
4 My mind _____ blank.
5 Before I realised what had _____, she/he'd …
6 I _____ _____ the number plate.
7 It all _____ so fast.
8 It _____ my mind that …
9 He/She looked as _____ …
10 He/She seemed _____ …

B Work in pairs. Choose one of the following incidents to report to the police and decide which sentences from Exercise 5A you could use.

- someone shoplifting in a department store
- someone looking at confidential information on someone else's computer
- someone hanging around an ATM with two friends sitting in a car nearby

C Work in pairs and take turns. Role-play the phone call. Student A: you are the police officer. Student B: you have seen the incident.

MOVING EXPERIENCES p116

POPULAR CULTURE p119

ON YOUR LEFT ... p122

THE PEOPLE'S PALACE p124

BBC INTERVIEWS

▷)) What area of the Arts do you enjoy?

10.1))) MOVING EXPERIENCES

G relative clauses
P intonation: relative clauses
V adjectives to describe films

VOCABULARY

ADJECTIVES TO DESCRIBE FILMS

1 A Work in pairs and discuss. Do you like the types of films shown in the photos? What types of films do you like?

B Work in pairs and check what you know. Cover Exercise 1C and complete the descriptions with a suitable adjective.

1 The documentary really made me think and raised lots of questions. It was …

2 I got lost sometimes – you had to pay attention to keep up with the plot and the action because it was so …

3 The relationship between the two people was sensitively handled and almost made me cry. It was very …

4 Some scenes were scary and made my skin crawl. It was …

5 I was on the edge of my seat and couldn't look away for a single moment. It was really …

6 The acting and direction were all exceptional, it'll win all the awards this year. It was absolutely …

7 I shouldn't be surprised if people start protests against this documentary. It's extremely …

8 There was a lot of violence and blood. For me it was just too …

9 We couldn't stop laughing, it was …

C Complete sentences 1–9 above with the words/ phrases a)–j). One item has two answers.

a) fast-paced
b) touching
c) gripping
d) gory
e) hysterical
f) creepy
g) controversial
h) full of suspense
i) outstanding
j) thought-provoking

D Check what you remember. Which adjectives in the box are synonyms or near-synonyms for the adjectives in Exercise 1C?

hilarious   moving   offensive   superb   dramatic
stunning   poignant   intense

2 A Work in groups. List the names of ten to fifteen films you all know.

B Take turns. Student A: describe one of the films using at least three of the adjectives from Exercise 1C. The other students: ask a *yes/no* question each and *then* guess the film.

A: It's fast-paced and the special effects are brilliant and some of it is gory.
B: Is it a thriller?
A: Yes.
C: Does it star … ?

LISTENING

3 A ▶ 10.1 Listen to someone talk about a film he never gets bored with watching. What is the film and what is the main reason he likes it?

B Listen again and make notes on the following:

1 why it's family-friendly

2 a memorable thing about the 'baddy'

3 where the film got its title

4 what the woman thinks about the film

5 examples of gripping moments

6 something unusual about the stunts

7 something the two people say about the heroine

8 the woman's preference in films

C Work in pairs and discuss. If you haven't seen the film, would you like to watch it based on this description? Is it true that there aren't many action films which include comedy?

4 A Work alone. Choose a film you never get bored with and make notes about:

• the actors.   • the plot.
• the setting.   • why you like it.

B Work in pairs. Tell each other about your film.

C Work with other students. Take turns telling each other about your choice. Which film you heard about would you most like to see?

GRAMMAR

RELATIVE CLAUSES

5 **A** Check what you know. Complete the online forum messages with *who, which, whose, where* or *when*.

What film do you never get bored with?

The *Shawshank Redemption* is a prison movie [1]_____ goes beyond the violence seen in most such films. The story centres on the life-changing relationship between a new prisoner, Andy (Tim Robbins), [2]_____ is imprisoned for murder, and Red (Morgan Freeman), a long-time prisoner [3]_____ he makes friends with. You really care about these two characters, [4]_____ unlikely friendship blossoms over the course of the film. I must have seen it twenty times and it's the one movie [5]_____ I never get bored with, especially Robbins' and Freeman's performances, for [6]_____, surprisingly, neither won a major award.

My all-time favourite is *Groundhog Day*, in [7]_____ Bill Murray relives one day over and over again. He plays Phil, a TV weatherman visiting a small U.S. town, [8]_____ he reports on a local annual festival. Phil detests the assignment and the local people, [9]_____ makes his situation even worse when he gets stuck with both. The story is endlessly inventive, by turns hilarious and poignant. It is especially touching in the moment [10]_____ Phil realises he loves Rita (Andie Macdowell) but can't win her, [11]_____ is a turning point in his transformation into a decent human being. He actually ends up loving the town [12]_____ inhabitants he initially despised. A classic!

B Work in pairs. Add *that* next to any relative pronouns which it could replace. Put brackets around relative pronouns that could be omitted.

C Complete the rules. Use the forum messages in Exercise 5A to help.

RULES

1 Defining relative clauses give *essential/extra* information about a person, thing, place or time. Non-defining relative clauses give *essential/extra* information.

2 The relative pronoun *that* can replace *who* or *which* in *defining/non-defining* clauses only.

3 The relative pronoun can be omitted when it is the *subject/object* of the verb in the relative clause.

4 Prepositions can come (a) at the *beginning/end* of a clause or (b) *before/after* the relative pronoun. *(a)/(b)* is more formal.

5 *What/Which* introducing a relative clause can be used to refer to the whole of a previous clause.

6 Commas are used before and after *defining/non-defining* clauses.

---

6 **A** Complete the forum message with commas.

It's a film which appeals to the teenage market and centres on the relationship between Bella who has just arrived in town and her mysterious classmate Edward whose family seems to have a strange secret. When Bella discovers Edward's true identity which happens about a third of the way through the film she has a big decision to make, a decision which will change her entire life.

B ▶ 10.2 **INTONATION: relative clauses** Listen to the intonation in the non-defining clauses. Are they higher or lower than the rest of the sentence?

C Listen again and say the recording at the same time, copying the intonation.

▷ page 136 **LANGUAGEBANK**

7 Combine the extracts from reviews using a relative clause.

1 The main role is played by Chiwetel Ejiofor. His portrayal of Solomon Northup earned him several awards.

2 Megastar Chris Hemsworth gives an emotional performance in his latest film. His career got its biggest boost from his role in *Thor*.

3 *Invictus* is a story about leadership and forgiveness at a critical period. Nelson Mandela had just become president of South Africa.

4 The film *Star Trek* was based on a popular TV series. William Shatner played the role of Captain Kirk in the series.

5 The film was Daniel Craig's third outing as James Bond. It was directed by Sam Mendes.

6 Adrian Brody shot to fame after starring in *The Pianist*. He won the Best Actor Oscar for this.

7 *Lost in Translation* takes place in a Tokyo hotel. The two main characters meet and form an unusual bond there.

8 *The Hurt Locker* is a war film directed by Kathryn Bigelow. The choice of Jordan as the filming location was important for her.

SPEAKING

8 **A** Complete the sentences below so that they are true for you.

I loathe films where …
I like the work of the director … , whose …
My favourite actress is … , who …
My favourite actor is … , who …
The film I most liked recently is …
I like it in films when …

B Work in pairs and take turns. Talk about your ideas and ask follow-up questions. Find out what you have in common.

MIDNIGHT IN PARIS

Midnight in Paris is set in Paris in the present and in different periods in the past. It stars Owen Wilson as Gil, a Hollywood screenwriter, and Rachel McAdams as Inez, his beautiful fiancée.

As the film opens, Gil is on holiday in Paris with Inez and her wealthy parents. He is supposed to be in love with his girlfriend but his love affair really seems to be with Paris in the springtime. One evening while wandering around the city, he gets lost and as the clock strikes midnight an old Peugeot car pulls up. Inside the car are a group of party-goers who are dressed in 1920s clothes and who invite him to join them. They go to a party where Gil realises he has been transported to the 1920s, a period which he loves. We see him meeting some of his intellectual and artistic heroes from that time and falling in love with Adriana, Picasso's mistress. Meanwhile, in the present, Gil's bride-to-be and her parents become more and more annoyed and suspicious about his nightly disappearances. Eventually Gil realises Inez is not right for him and breaks up with her. He decides to stay and live in his beloved Paris.

Skilfully directed by Woody Allen, the film cuts between the glitter of Paris in the twenties and the present-day city. The script is alternately gripping, shocking and hilarious and the camerawork is stunning. As Gil, Owen Wilson is appealing in his enthusiasm and love of Paris in the past. However, for me, it is the character of Adriana, convincingly acted by Marion Cotillard, who is the most fascinating of all.

With its charm, sparkling wit and engaging leaps forwards and backwards in time, *Midnight in Paris* is a light, delightful film which I'd thoroughly recommend.

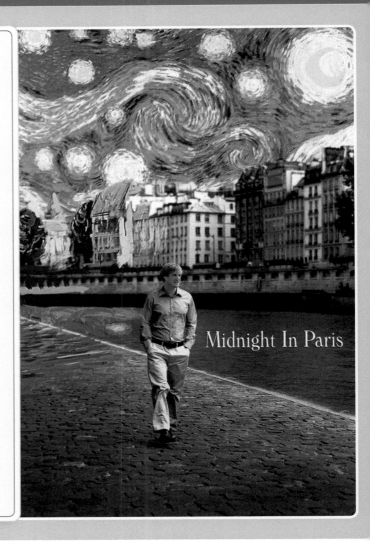

Midnight In Paris

WRITING

A REVIEW; LEARN TO USE ADVERB + PAST PARTICIPLE COMBINATIONS

9 A Work in pairs and discuss the questions.

1 Where do you usually read film reviews (e.g. on the internet, in magazines)?

2 What is the <u>main</u> purpose of a film review?
   • to make people want to see the film
   • to help people decide if they want to see a film
   • to give factual information about the film

3 Which of the topics in the box do you usually find in a film review?

> plot summary   description of the film's ending
> actors' names   recommendation
> ticket prices   setting of the film
> reviewer's opinion of different elements

B Read the film review above. Would you like to see the film? Why/Why not?

C Read the review again and write the topic of each paragraph. Use the topics in the box to help.

10 A Underline two adverb + past participle combinations in paragraph 3 of the review.

B Write three adverbs from the box next to each participle to complete the phrases. Some can be used more than once.

> convincingly   harshly   skilfully   widely
> sensitively   overwhelmingly   highly
> poignantly   heavily

1 _____ / _____ / _____ directed by …
2 _____ / _____ / _____ acted by …
3 _____ / _____ / _____ praised by …
4 _____ / _____ / _____ criticised by …

11 A Make notes about a film you have seen recently or a film you never get bored with. Use the topic areas from Exercise 9C.

B Write a first draft of your review (120–180 words). Use adjectives and at least two adverb + past participle combinations.

C Exchange with another student and read each other's review. Is it interesting and clear? Suggest two or three improvements.

D Write a final version of the review.

G participle clauses
P word stress; connected speech
V the Arts; two-part phrases

((**10.2**

READING

1 A Work in pairs and look at the photos. What do you think is the most difficult part of each performer's job?

B Work in pairs and discuss these questions from a magazine article. Make notes on your answers.

1 How do actors cry on demand?
2 Do big stars have to audition for film roles?
3 How do singers keep their voices steady when they're dancing?
4 Why is rock music played so loud at concerts?
5 Who decides whether something is 'art' or not?
6 Why do works of art get stolen if they can't be sold without attracting attention?
7 What's the secret to making an audience laugh?
8 How does a comedian deal with hecklers?

C Work in pairs. Student A: turn to page 145. Student B: quickly read the text on this page. Which four questions above does it answer?

D Read the text again. Write a maximum of five key words for each answer to help you remember the information.

E Work in pairs. Cover the text and look at your notes from Exercise 1D. Tell your partner about the answers.

POPULAR CULTURE

**Want to know the best-kept secrets of popular culture?
Read our Top Questions & Answers to find out.**

Q:

A: Rock music is characterised by a strong bass line and hard, driving rhythm and percussion parts, which are greatly enhanced by amplification. At some point in the evolution of rock, audiences became almost addicted to the sensations of the music they loved 'vibrating' inside them at concerts. The listeners go beyond hearing the music and feel it through their whole body, feel its vibrations, provided it is loud enough. Heavy metal music played softly sounds stupid and can only be played as it was intended to be: very, very loudly.

Q:

A: A big star auditioning for a part is almost unheard of. Actors such as Tom Hanks go straight from film to film, so directors and producers have access to a whole portfolio of their work. The closest such actors ever get to anything resembling an audition is when they're invited to chat about the project informally, which gives the director and producer a chance to evaluate the actor without it feeling like a test. The stars don't usually even have to read part of the script. More often, it's actually a matter of the actor choosing whether to work with the director!

Q:

A: Every stand-up comedian knows that making people laugh with prepared material, on stage, is very different from making your friends or colleagues laugh in an informal setting. You need to focus on technique, such as which words to stress, when to pause, how to use facial expressions and body movements, as well as sensing how to work each individual audience. Interestingly, shows with paying audiences are better than freebies. Having paid to be entertained, people are often more ready and willing to laugh.

Q:

A: Criminals steal paintings only when they already have a buyer. Sometimes, a wealthy private collector actually requests a particular piece to be stolen – essentially orders it – for part of their private collection. The collector knows that it can never be shown publicly but that's not why they want the piece in the first place. Valuable works of art are a favourite commodity for criminal organisations, who will use them in place of cash for making deals with each other. They are also useful for money launderers, as works of art are easier to transport and harder to trace than cash, as well as easily traded on the black market.

GRAMMAR

PARTICIPLE CLAUSES

2 **A** Read the article below. In what situations do celebrities use fake names? What is the joke in each chosen name?

Do stars use their real names when travelling?

In short, no. In fact, stars ¹**registered at hotels under their real name** are a rarity – their day can be ruined by paparazzi ²**trying to take their pictures** and members of the public ³**taking selfies**. So if you're going to change your name, why not have fun doing it? Names ⁴**involving wordplay** are common: Britney Spears uses Ms Alotta Warmheart among other names, and Brad Pitt and Jennifer Aniston, ⁵**married in 2000 but divorced five years later**, used to call themselves Mr and Mrs Ross Vegas. And the fun doesn't end there – the name ⁶**used by George Clooney** when he was travelling caused him great amusement: Arnold Schwarzenegger. 'It was funny, the hotel staff had to call me Mr Schwarzenegger, when they knew of course, I wasn't him,' said Clooney.

B Work in pairs and look at the participle clauses in bold in the article. Then answer the questions.

1 Which participle clauses in bold replace relative clauses?
2 What is the full relative clause in each case?
3 Which two verb forms can a participle clause begin with?

C Compare the sentences below and underline the participle clauses. Then complete the rule.

1 **a)** Names which involve wordplay are common.
  b) Names involving wordplay are common.
2 **a)** The people who worked in the hotel thought the name was funny.
  b) The people working in the hotel thought the name was funny.
3 **a)** The hotel, which was built in the 1980s and which is often used by film stars, is famous.
  b) The hotel, built in the 1980s and regularly used by film stars, is famous.

RULES	
	1 When a relative clause has an active verb in the present simple or past simple, the participle clause uses a _____ participle.
	2 When a relative clause has a passive verb in the present simple or past simple, the participle clause uses a _____ participle.

speakout TIP

Using participle clauses can improve the level of your writing and speaking. Try to improve this sentence by using a participle clause: *I couldn't concentrate on the concert because there were so many people who took photos.*

▷ page 136 **LANGUAGEBANK**

---

3 **A** Rewrite the sentences using a participle clause.

1 People who take photos should ask their subjects' permission first.
2 Films that are based on books are disappointing.
3 It's great to see rock stars in their sixties who still play concerts.
4 Architecture which was designed in the 1960s is generally quite ugly and ought to be pulled down.
5 Photos of people who are posing for the camera don't work as well as spontaneous pictures.
6 Film and TV stars who appear at the theatre attract huge audiences.
7 Jokes which involve racial stereotypes are not funny.
8 Photographers who used software to enhance their photos were justifiably banned from entering a national competition last month.

B Work in pairs and discuss. Do you agree with the statements in Exercise 3A? Give examples.

VOCABULARY

THE ARTS

4 **A** Which of the forum comments are generally positive (✓), negative (✗) or mixed (–)?

❝ I'd read a lot about this new singer in the music press. She's certainly **creating a stir** with her **ground-breaking** mix of rap and folk. Ever since she got those **rave reviews** in the press, each performance has been a **sell-out** and it's impossible to get tickets. Everyone says it's the **must-see** performance of the year. Is she really that good? ❞

❝ Well, after all the **hype** surrounding her concerts, I went to see her on Friday, expecting something really sensational … but the concert was a real **letdown**! It was a complete **flop** because we couldn't hear her properly. ❞

❝ Yeah, I was at that gig and the technical side was pretty bad but her album is amazing, really innovative. I've never heard anything quite like it before. I just hope she doesn't go **mainstream** and boring like all the other **alternative** artists. ❞

B Work in pairs. What do you think the words and phrases in bold above mean? Use the context, grammar and your knowledge of similar words to help. Then check in a dictionary.

C ▶ 10.3 WORD STRESS Work in pairs and say the words and phrases in bold. Which syllable(s) is/are stressed? Listen to the words in context and check.

D Think of a performance you have seen or heard. Write a forum entry about it using at least four of the words which are new to you.

E Read other students' forum entries. Find a performance you would like to see or hear.

▷ page 142 **VOCABULARYBANK**

SPEAKING

5 A Choose three of the questions below to answer. Write the name of the thing/person and two or three words to explain why you liked it/him/her.

1 What's the best gig/concert or dance performance you've ever been to?

2 What's the best music album ever made?

3 Who's the funniest comedian you know?

4 What's the most moving, scary or exciting film you've ever seen?

5 What's the most memorable exhibition you've ever been to?

6 What's the best photo you've ever taken?

7 Who's the painter or other type of artist you most like? What's your favourite work of his/hers?

8 What's the most unforgettable show or play you've ever seen?

B Work in pairs and take turns. Talk about your experiences and feelings.

C Work in groups and take turns. Recommend something you've recently been to/seen/heard.

VOCABULARY *PLUS*

TWO-PART PHRASES

6 A Work in pairs and look at the two-part phrases in sentences 1 and 2. What do you think they mean?

1 There are some basic **dos and don'ts** when taking a good photo.

2 I've worked in the film business **off and on** for most of my life.

B Check your ideas with the dictionary entries.

D **dos and don'ts** things that you should and should not do: *the dos and don'ts of having a pet*

O **off and on/on and off** for short periods of time but not regularly: *I worked as a secretary off and on for three years.*

From Longman Active Study Dictionary.

7 A Match a word from A with one from B to make a two-part phrase.

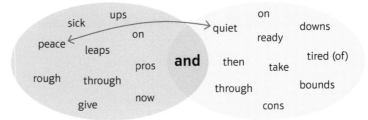

B ▶ **10.4** **CONNECTED SPEECH** Listen and check. Then listen and repeat, paying attention to the linking, the weak form of *and* /ən/ and the dropping of /d/ in connected speech.

ups͜ and̶ downs

8 A Work in pairs. Student A: turn to page 145. Student B: turn to page 143. Read the definitions and then complete five of the sentences below.

1 I hate having music on in the background. I prefer some _____ and _____.

2 I used to go to rock concerts a lot but nowadays I only go _____ and _____.

3 I'm a reggae fan _____ and _____.

4 I'm _____ and _____ of having to listen to people's favourite music on the train. I wish they'd turn their MP3 players down.

5 Any skill such as playing the piano improves in _____ and _____ if you practise enough.

6 Every relationship has its _____ and _____ so it's not surprising that most bands break up after a few years.

7 I don't like jazz. Some of the pieces go _____ and _____ for far too long.

8 It's OK for my neighbours to play music I don't like. You have to have a bit of _____ and _____. I'm sure they don't like my music!

9 There are _____ and _____ to listening to a live recording as opposed to a studio album.

10 Some of the music videos made by ordinary people on *YouTube* are a bit _____ and _____ but that's OK.

B Work in pairs and take turns. Help your partner to complete the sentences and understand the two-part phrases.

C Change five of the sentences so that they are true for you. Then compare with a partner. How many do you agree on?

▷ page 142 **VOCABULARYBANK**

F giving a tour
P intonation in comments
V dimensions

A   B   C   D

Greenwich Village, New York, USA

SPEAKING

1 Work in pairs and discuss the questions.

1 Have you ever shown anyone around your town/city?

2 What places of interest in your town/city you would take a visitor to? Why?

FUNCTION

GIVING A TOUR

2 A Work in pairs. Look at the photos of Greenwich Village and Oxford and discuss. What do you know about each place? Which would you most like to visit?

B ▶ 10.5 Listen to two people showing visitors around Greenwich Village and Oxford. Number the photos in the order you hear them.

C Listen again and write one fact you hear about each place.

1 The Blue Note Jazz Club
2 The Café Reggio
3 Greenwich Village in general
4 Washington Square Park
5 The Bodleian Library
6 The Oxford colleges
7 The Bridge of Sighs
8 New College
9 The 'Schools'
10 Christ Church College

3 A Work in pairs and complete the phrases. Sometimes there is more than one possible answer.

Leading the way

Let's ¹_____ over to Washington Square Park and then ²_____ back.

Why don't we ³_____ our steps and go back to the Café Reggio?

Giving facts

It was ⁴_____ on the Arc de Triomphe.

It was built to ⁵_____ the hundredth anniversary of the inauguration of George Washington as president.

In front of us is the Bodleian, ⁶_____ after the ⁷_____ – Thomas Bodley.

Commenting on facts

⁸_____ I'm sure you ⁹_____, Greenwich Village has always been a centre of artistic life – very bohemian.

¹⁰_____, the oldest college was actually only founded a hundred or so years earlier!

¹¹_____, the biggest room can seat somewhere in the region of 500 students although I haven't seen it myself.

We can actually go inside if we're quick. It's well ¹²_____ a visit.

B Compare your answers with the audio script on page 153.

C ▶ 10.6 INTONATION IN COMMENTS Listen to the intonation in the phrases. Then listen again and repeat.

Interestingly, the statue disappeared at the time of his death.

The story goes, he threw it in the lake.

Apparently, it was made of gold.

Surprisingly, no one has ever tried to find it.

▷ page 136 **LANGUAGEBANK**

Oxford, England

4 A Complete A's part in the extracts from a tour of Paris.

A: ¹Let's / head / over / the cathedral, Notre Dame.
B: On the island? Do we have time to go inside?
A: ²Yes, / well worth / visit it.

B: … So that's the Arc de Triomphe?
A: ³Yes, / model / a famous Roman arch.
B: And why was it built?
A: ⁴celebrate / one / Napoleon's great victories.

A: ⁵ … So here we are / the Eiffel Tower / named / its designer, Gustave Eiffel.
B: Wow! It's impressive.
A: ⁶Yeah / apparently / can sway six to seven centimetres in the wind!

B Work in pairs and take turns. Practise the conversations using the prompts above.

VOCABULARY

DIMENSIONS

5 Complete the tourist's questions with the noun or verb form of the adjectives in brackets.

1 What is the _____ of the tower? (high)
2 So the road goes the _____ of the town? (long)
3 When did they _____ the entrance? (wide)
4 What is the _____ of the wall here? (thick)
5 The road _____ here. Why's that? (narrow)
6 What's the _____ of the river and _____ of the water here? (broad, deep)
7 Why don't they _____ the map? It's so small. (large)
8 It's nine o'clock and it's still light. When do the days _____ here? (short)

LEARN TO

EXPRESS ESTIMATES

6 A Look at the extracts and underline five phrases for expressing estimates (when we don't know the exact number).

1 **A:** How many colleges are there?
  B: Just under forty. Well, thirty-eight to be exact.
2 **A:** How 'new' is new?
  B: Roughly 1370.
  A: You're kidding!
  B: No, really! Interestingly, the oldest college was actually only founded a hundred or so years earlier!
3 Apparently, the biggest room can seat somewhere in the region of five hundred students.
4 **A:** How many students are there at the university in total?
  B: To be honest, it depends. In term time, you'd probably get upwards of twenty thousand.

B Which phrases in Exercise 6A could be replaced by 1) *fewer than*, 2) *more than* or 3) *about/around/approximately*?

C ▶ 10.7 Listen and tick the exact number.

1 **a)** 1,400   **b)** 1,518
2 **a)** 30   **b)** 38
3 **a)** 1,180   **b)** 1,220
4 **a)** 712   **b)** 746
5 **a)** 2.13   **b)** 1.10
6 **a)** 318   **b)** 371

D Work in pairs and take turns to estimate:
• the number of students in your school/employees in your workplace.
• the age of the building you're in.
• the population of your town/city.
• the distance from your home to where you are now.
• the cost of dinner in a good restaurant in your town/city.
• the number of contacts on your mobile phone.
• the number of English words you know.

SPEAKING

7 A Work in pairs. Design a one-hour walking or cycling tour of a town/city you know for a visitor. Make notes on:

• four or five places to see.
• a fact or personal opinion about each place.
• some approximate numbers associated with the place (how many people visit it; how much it costs; how old/long/high, etc. it is).

B Work with a new partner and take turns. Role-play the tour. Student A: lead the way. Student B: ask questions.

DVD PREVIEW

1 A Look at the photos of a new library and discuss the questions in pairs.

1 Which words/phrases in the box would you use to describe the building?

> crazy   makes a bold statement   unique   fresh
> pleasing on the eye   modern   too busy   delicate
> too elaborate   beautiful   amazing   unsightly

2 How is it different from what you expect a library to look like?

3 What facilities would you expect to be included in a 21ˢᵗ-century library?

B Read the programme information and look at the photos. Which of the following do you think you will see in the DVD?

1 The reporter interviews local people, the designer of the building and celebrities.

2 The designer explains why she used rings as part of the design.

3 The local people feel mostly positive about the new library.

◀)) The Culture Show: ⒷⒷⒸ The People's Palace

At a time when many libraries across Britain face budget cuts and closure, Birmingham is opening the biggest public library in Europe. Is this a new breed of super library for the future?

This programme explores the cutting-edge building to discover what a 21st-century library looks like, what goes into its design, and how local people – the taxpayers – feel about it. Perhaps most importantly, we find out what role the library has in the internet age.

DVD VIEW

2 A Watch the DVD and check your answers to Exercise 1B.

B Work in pairs and answer the questions. Then watch the DVD again and check.

1 Why and how is Birmingham regenerating its city centre?

2 How does the designer describe the city of Birmingham? What characteristics did she try to reflect in the library's design?

3 Why did she call it a 'People's Palace'?

4 What is there inside the library besides shelves of books?

5 What is the 'façade bench' and what can you do there?

6 What do people say they like once they're inside the library?

C Watch the DVD again and underline the correct alternative.

1 We started with this idea, that's the *tradition/ heritage* of the proud industrial city, with the steel industry.

2 I think any *funding/investment* of money put into libraries at the moment is fantastic.

3 And in a time of economic *austerity/strictness*, what a bold step to take. Wonderful stuff!

4 There's a lot of people, students, they want to be *independent/individual* but be part of a bigger collective.

5 It's brilliant, yeah, I really like it, it's very *user-friendly/easy-to-use*.

6 I love this *in particular/especially*. I love this outside *bit/section* with the balcony.

3 Work in pairs and discuss whether you agree/ disagree with the statements.

1 Local governments shouldn't spend taxpayer's money on expensive architecture.

2 Libraries still have an important role in the internet age.

3 For a society to be healthy, it needs public spaces like libraries, parks and theatres.

speakout a town project

4 A ▶ **10.8** Listen to three people discussing a new public space or artistic project for their town. Which project does each person, Tim, Nigel and Sarah, like from the list below? Why?

- an outdoor sculpture (modern or traditional)
- a concert space
- a theatre workshop space for young people
- a state-of-the-art multiplex cinema
- a botanical garden
- a skateboarding park

B Listen again and tick the key phrases you hear.

> **KEY PHRASES**
>
> I'm really in favour of the …
>
> I think that it would be [beneficial for the community/popular/ …].
>
> The only thing that would concern me though is that …
>
> I'd rather have something that would [appeal to all ages/make a statement/…]
>
> We have to consider [costs/maintenance/ …]
>
> Can you see the [older/younger] generation [using/liking] it?

5 A Work in pairs. You are responsible for choosing an artistic project for your town/city. Choose two items from the list in Exercise 4A. The items must:

- have artistic and/or architectural merit.
- represent the town/city in some way.
- convey a positive image.

B Work with other students. Discuss your ideas and decide on one project.

C Present your decision to the class.

writeback a work of art

6 A Work in pairs. Read about the competition and tell your partner what you would choose and why.

> We want you to write about a favourite work of art or building. It could be a statue or sculpture, a fountain or bridge, a painting or even a favourite room. Send us your description in 150–250 words, and we'll put the five best entries on our website.

B Read the description and tick (✓) the topics in the box that the writer mentions.

> setting   when it was made   material   colour
> size   who made it   why he/she likes it

> My favourite building is in fact a bridge, the Millau Viaduct in southern France. It's an awe-inspiring structure, as much a work of art as it is a bridge. It towers over the valley that it crosses, but is so graceful that it seems to me more an integral part of the natural environment than the architectural and engineering achievement that it is.
>
> It was designed by a French engineer and a British architect who conceived it as a series of towers, which look like the masts of a ship, from which cables are suspended, the cables that support the road surface that runs 2500 metres across the valley. The highest tower is the tallest structure in France, taller than the Eiffel Tower, and I think the tallest bridge in the world.
>
> This 21st-century masterpiece is breathtaking to behold, and it gives me a sense of calm every time I look at it. No one should miss it if they are visiting this part of France.

C Write your competition entry. Use the box in Exercise 6B for ideas of what to include.

D Read your classmates' competition entries. Which one makes you most want to visit the place they write about?

125

Ⓥ ADJECTIVES

1 A Work in pairs. Make a list of as many adjectives for describing films as you can remember.

B Complete comments 1–4 with a suitable adjective.

1 The ending was sensitively handled and made me cry! Very _____!

2 The script was basically one joke after another. Absolutely _____!

3 It kept my attention for two hours. Utterly _____!

4 My friends and I are still arguing about it. Quite _____!

C Work in pairs. Write four review comments similar to the ones above. Use a suitable adjective for describing films in each review.

Ⓖ RELATIVE CLAUSES

2 A Underline the correct alternative.

I'd like to find …

1 a person *who/for whom/whose* main interests include **doing sports**.

2 a place *that/which/where* I can **speak English with native speakers**.

3 someone *that/whose/whom* knows **a famous person**.

4 a shop *where/which/that* I can buy **reasonably priced clothes**.

5 a person for *whose/that/whom* **money** is not important.

6 three **interesting places in this town/city** *which/to which/where* I've never been to.

B Change the words in bold in four of the sentences above so that they are about things/people you'd like to find.

C Ask other students questions about your sentences in Exercise 2B.

A: Do you know anyone whose main interests include going to the cinema?
B: Yes – me.
A: Right. Who's your favourite actor?
B: At the moment, Christian Bale.

Ⓖ PARTICIPLE CLAUSES

3 A Complete the quiz with the present or past participles of the verbs in brackets.

Trivia quiz

1 It's an arts building _____ (stand) in Sydney Harbour and _____ (make) of white tiles to look like sails.

2 It's a company _____ (start) by Steve Jobs, Steve Wozniak and Ronald Wayne, best _____ (know) for its iPod and iPhone products.

3 It's a game _____ (play) by two players, _____ (involve) a small rubber ball and racquets and _____ (take) place in a four-walled court indoors.

4 He was a great leader, born in Corsica, _____ (crown) Emperor of France in 1804 and _____ (defeat) at Waterloo in 1815.

5 It's a statuette _____ (award) to people in the film world every year by the American Academy of Motion Picture Arts and Sciences.

6 They're a group of people _____ (live) in cold, snowy parts of the USA and Canada, and _____ (use) blocks of ice to build their houses, _____ (call) igloos.

7 It's a Japanese dish _____ (consist) of raw fish and rice _____ (roll) up in seaweed.

8 It's a play _____ (write) by Shakespeare and _____ (feature) a Danish prince.

B Work in pairs and do the quiz.

C Check your answers on page 143.

Ⓥ THE ARTS

4 The words in bold are in the wrong sentences. Put them in the correct sentences.

1 The musical was a complete **sell-out** and had to close early.

2 Does the Picasso exhibition deserve all those **hype** reviews?

3 The new sculpture is **alternative**. Everyone's arguing about it.

4 He's famous for his **mainstream** work in photography, never done before.

5 You can't get tickets for the show. It's a complete **rave**.

6 I thought the new album was a real **must-see**, very poor.

7 That new comedian is certainly creating a lot of **flop**. Everyone's talking about him.

8 This Virtual Worlds Exhibition is a **letdown** event. Don't miss it!

9 I don't listen to **ground-breaking** pop music much. It all sounds the same.

10 During **creating a stir** Fashion Week you can see some shockingly original clothes.

Ⓕ GIVING A TOUR

5 A Complete descriptions 1–3 below with the words in the box. Where are the places?

~~was~~   story   worth   it   you   honour   named   rebuilt

was

1 It built in the 17th century by Shah Jahan in of his wife. As may know, it's made of white marble and is well a visit.

2 It was after its designer and was built in 1889. The goes that many Parisians hated it because it was too modern.

3 Parts of it were many times. Believe or not, millions of Chinese died in its construction.

B Write two sentences about a tourist site you know.

C Read out your sentences. The other students guess the place.

IRREGULAR VERBS

Verb	Past simple	Past participle
be	was	been
beat	beat	beaten
become	became	become
begin	began	begun
bend	bent	bent
bet	bet	bet
bite	bit	bitten
bleed	bled	bled
blow	blew	blown
break	broke	broken
bring	brought	brought
broadcast	broadcast	broadcast
build	built	built
burn	burned/burnt	burned/burnt
burst	burst	burst
buy	bought	bought
catch	caught	caught
choose	chose	chosen
come	came	come
cost	cost	cost
cut	cut	cut
deal	dealt	dealt
dig	dig	dug
do	did	done
draw	drew	drawn
dream	dreamed/dreamt	dreamed/dreamt
drink	drank	drunk
drive	drove	driven
eat	ate	eaten
fall	fell	fallen
feel	felt	felt
feed	fed	fed
fight	fought	fought
find	found	found
fly	flew	flown
forbid	forbade	forbidden
forget	forgot	forgotten
forgive	forgave	forgiven
freeze	froze	frozen
get	got	got
give	gave	given
go	went	gone
grow	grew	grown
hang	hung	hung
have	had	had
hear	heard	heard
hide	hid	hidden
hit	hit	hit
hold	held	held
hurt	hurt	hurt
keep	kept	kept
know	knew	known
lay	laid	laid
lead	led	led
leap	leapt	leapt
lean	leaned/leant	leaned/leant
learn	learned/learnt	learned/learnt

Verb	Past simple	Past participle
leave	left	left
lend	lent	lent
let	let	let
lie	lay	lain
light	lit	lit
lose	lost	lost
make	made	made
mean	meant	meant
meet	met	met
mistake	mistook	mistaken
pay	paid	paid
put	put	put
read	read	read
ride	rode	ridden
ring	rang	rung
rise	rose	risen
run	ran	run
say	said	said
see	saw	seen
sell	sold	sold
send	sent	sent
set	set	set
shake	shook	shaken
shine	shone	shone
shoot	shot	shot
show	showed	shown
shrink	shrank	shrunk
shut	shut	shut
sing	sang	sung
sink	sank	sunk
sit	sat	sat
sleep	slept	slept
slide	slid	slid
smell	smelled/smelt	smelled/smelt
speak	spoke	spoken
spell	spelt	spelt
spend	spent	spent
spill	spilled/spilt	spilled/spilt
split	split	split
spread	spread	spread
stand	stood	stood
steal	stole	stolen
stick	stuck	stuck
sting	stung	stung
swim	swam	swum
take	took	taken
teach	taught	taught
tear	tore	torn
tell	told	told
think	thought	thought
throw	threw	thrown
understand	understood	understood
wake	woke	woken
wear	wore	worn
win	won	won
write	wrote	written

GRAMMAR

6.1 modal verbs and related phrases

	present	past
obligation (strong)	have to go must go make someone go	had to go – made someone go
obligation (mild)	should go ought to go am supposed to go	should have gone ought to have gone was supposed to go
lack of obligation	don't have to go	didn't have to go
prohibition (strong)	mustn't go can't go am not allowed to go	– couldn't go wasn't allowed to go
prohibition (mild)	shouldn't go oughtn't to go am not supposed to go	shouldn't have gone oughtn't to have gone wasn't supposed to go
permission	can go am allowed to go may go let someone go	could go was allowed to go might go let someone go
ability	can/can't go am/am not able to go manage/ don't manage to go	could/couldn't go was/wasn't able to go managed/ didn't manage to go

obligation

Must can express that the obligation is internal, not (only) because of a rule.

*I **must** finish this report – I don't want to annoy the boss.*

Use *make someone do something* when someone forces another person to do something.

*My mum **makes** me study for two hours every night.*

Use *be supposed to* especially when the obligation is broken.

*I'm not **supposed** to eat chocolate but …*

lack of obligation/prohibition

Note the difference between *don't have to* and *mustn't*:

*You **don't have to** arrive before 5p.m.* (it's not necessary)
*You **mustn't** arrive before 5p.m.* (you're not allowed to)

permission

Use *let + someone* or *allow someone to* to say that someone gave permission to someone.

*Do you think she'll **let** me take a day off?*
*My company **allows us** to work from home one day a week.*

ability

For ability on a single occasion in the past, use *was/were able to* or *managed to* (not *could*).

*He **was able to** find his way out of the forest and get help.*
NOT *He could find his way …*

Use *manage to* for something that is/was difficult to do.

*He **managed to** run the race in under three hours.*

6.2 future perfect and continuous

future continuous

Use *will + be + -ing* form for:

* something that will be in progress at or around a specific future time.

you call

now

d r i v i n g

*I'll **be driving** home when you call, so just leave a message.*

* something that will happen in the normal course of events, not as part of a particular intention or plan.

*I expect I'll **be talking** to Ian tomorrow, so I could ask him then.*

Note: We can use this meaning to introduce requests in a neutral way.

*A: Will you **be passing** the postbox?*
B: Yes.
A: In that case, could you post this for me?

future perfect

Use *will + have +* past participle to talk about something that will finish before a specific time in the future, often with the preposition *by*, meaning *at the latest*.

*I'll **have finished** this report by the end of the week.*

finish the report

now   ? ? ? ?   the end of the week

It's possible to use other modals, adverbs and phrases with both forms.

I might have finished/I definitely won't have finished/ I'd like to have finished by then.

*This time next week **I could be relaxing/I'll probably be relaxing/I'd like to be relaxing** on a beach.*

6.3 persuading

Use the following phrases to persuade someone by giving a strong opinion:

Surely Clearly Anyone can see that	parents need to take more responsibility for their kids' education.

Use negative questions when you want to persuade someone by inviting them to agree with you.

Don't you agree/think (that) Isn't it true/obvious that	texting is harmful for children's writing?
Shouldn't people Doesn't she want to	spend more time at home?

PRACTICE

6.1

A Underline the correct alternatives in the blog.

HOME » TRAVEL

Traveller's journal – Changing times

... it was the 1980s and travel there was very restricted back then. Of course you [1]*had to/must* get a visa to enter the country as well as a permit to travel to most cities. Or at least you [2]*should/were supposed to* get a permit; I didn't always get one, and once without a permit I [3]*could/managed to* go to a town that foreigners technically [4]*couldn't/didn't have to* go to. The police called me in and [5]*made/let* me answer questions. I spoke the language a little so I was [6]*able to/allowed to* communicate with them. Once they were convinced that I wasn't a spy, they [7]*allowed/let* me go and I was [8]*allowed to/able* stay there as long as I wanted. Of course, it's changed so much now. You still [9]*must/have to* get a visa to enter, but you [10]*mustn't/don't have to* get a permit to go anywhere within the country. As was always the case, if you [11]*are able/can* speak the language, it's a really enriching experience, and I think everyone [12]*ought to/is supposed to* try to spend at least a few weeks travelling there.

B Rewrite the sentences. Use the word in brackets so that the meaning stays the same.

1 I fell asleep. It was difficult. (manage)
   I _____.
2 We stayed for dinner. There was no choice. (to)
   We _____.
3 He gave me permission to listen to my MP3 player. (let)
   He _____.
4 It was too dark to see anything. (not able)
   He _____.
5 It's a good idea for her to leave before dark. (ought)
   She _____.
6 The rule was to pay before going in. We didn't pay at all. (suppose)
   We _____.
7 The maximum age to enter this disco is eighteen. (not allow)
   Adults _____.
8 I had to change my passport photo. (make)
   They _____.

6.2

A Complete the sentences with the future perfect or the future continuous form of the verb in brackets.

1 The film starts at eight, and it's about two hours long.
   At nine, I _____ the film. (watch)
   By eleven, the film _____. (finish)
2 Her plane lands at 11.45p.m.
   At midnight she _____ for her luggage. (probably/wait)
   By the time we wake up tomorrow, she _____ in Madrid. (arrive)
3 The world hotdog-eating champion can eat more than six hotdogs a minute.
   In ten minutes from now, he _____ over sixty hotdogs. (eat)
   Tonight in his sleep, he _____ about hotdogs! (dream)
4 Give me a day to think about it.
   By this time tomorrow, I _____. (decide)
   This time next week, I _____ I had decided differently. (wish)

B Find and correct the mistakes in A's part of the conversations.

Conversation 1
A: [1]Will you seeing Frank today?
B: Yes, do you want me to give him a message?
A: [2]Yes, could you tell him I won't probably have finished the report until tomorrow.

Conversation 2
A: [3]Just think – this time tomorrow you'll finish all your exams.
B: I know. That's what keeps me going.
A: [4]And you be celebrating with your friends.

Conversation 3
A: [5]Will you use your computer at lunchtime today? I've got a problem with mine.
B: No, I'm going out and I won't be back till four if you want to use it till then.
A: [6]I might still using it when you get back. The technicians might not have fixed mine by then.

6.3

A Use the prompts to complete the sentences. Use negative questions where appropriate.

A: [1]Do / agree / people / should / able / start a family when they're teenagers?
   Don't you agree that people should be able to start ...
B: What, even at 16 or 17?
A: Yes. [2]Clear / they at the peak of their physical health.
B: [3]But / is / it / obvious / most / 17-year-olds aren't even mature enough to be responsible for themselves?

A: Yeah, [4]but does / depend / the individual? Some 18-year-olds might make good parents.
B: [5]But / sure / they / need / time to sort out their own lives first.
A: [6]But / is / it / fact / that in some cultures 18 is a normal age to have a family?
B: Yes, [7]but / anyone / see / that what works in one culture won't necessarily work in every culture.
A: Hmm. Maybe you're right.

GRAMMAR

7.1 quantifiers

	100%	a large amount	a small amount	0%
uncountable or plural nouns	all, any	a lot of, lots of, plenty of, most	some, hardly any	no, not any
uncountable nouns		much, a large amount of, a great deal of	a little, little	
plural nouns	both (= all of two)	many, a large number of, quite a few	several, a small number of, a few, few	
singular nouns	each, every, any			no, not any, neither (= none of two)

a few/a little = some or a small amount
*There's still **a little** butter left.*

few/little = not many/much or not as many/ much as wanted or expected
*Very **few** people came to the meeting.*

any = It doesn't matter which/who
*I like **any** brand(s) of chocolate.*

Any is stressed.

Use *both* + plural verb, *neither* + singular verb.
***Both** of us **run** a business but **neither** of us **is** good with numbers.*

Another + singular nouns and numbers = something is additional to the existing number.
*Could I have **another** piece of cake, please.*
*We've got **another** three meetings today.*

Use the pronoun *none* for a short answer.
*How much sugar have we got? **None**.*

7.2 reported speech

In reported speech, the original verb form often goes back further into the past. Pronouns, time references, etc. also change.

direct speech	reported speech
present simple/continuous *'I want to be a chef.'* *'We're working.'*	past simple/continuous *He said he wanted to be a chef.* *She told me they were working.*
past simple/present perfect *'Ben phoned me last week.'* *'I've read your book.'*	past perfect *She told me Ben had phoned her the week before.* *He said he'd read my book.*
will/would/can/could/ should *'We'll help you tomorrow.'* *'You can stay with me.'*	would/could/should *He said they'd help me the next day.* *She said I could stay with her.*

It is not necessary to change the verb form when reporting something that is still true now or was said very recently.
'It's going to rain.' Sam's just said it's going to rain.

reported questions
Use normal statement word order without *do/does/did* or a question mark.
*'What does Ian think?' She asked me **what Ian thought**.*
NOT ~~She asked me what did Ian think.~~
With *yes/no* questions, use *if* or *whether*.
*'Are you OK?' She asked **if** I was OK.*
Also use *wanted to know, enquired* and *wondered*.
*They **wanted to know** what time the train left.*

reported requests
Use verb + object + infinitive with *to*.
*'Could you sing?' He asked us **to sing**.*

time phrases and place references
Time phrases and place references usually change.
now → then/at that time
yesterday → the day before/previous day
tomorrow → the following/next day
a week ago → the week before
here → there

7.3 adding emphasis

auxiliary verbs	
add or stress auxiliaries	I **do** hate it when people smoke indoors. It **is** annoying.

intensifiers	
really, so + any adjective or adverb	It's **so** outrageous. You play **really well**.
absolutely, completely, totally + extreme adjectives	It's **completely** ridiculous.
such (a/an) + (adjective) + noun	It'll be **such an** amazing day. It was **such** terrible weather.

emphasising phrases	
pronoun/noun + *be* + *the one who*	**You're the one who** chose it.
the + adjective + *thing* + *be*	**The best thing was** the music.

informal phrases	
There's no way (that) …	**There's no way** Tom stole the money.
What/Who/ Where/Why/ How on earth … ?	**Why on earth** didn't you say? **Where on earth** did you buy that?

PRACTICE

7.1 **A** Underline the correct alternative.

What does your ringtone say about you?

Almost everyone now has a mobile phone and ¹*a great deal/ a large number/the most* of us have our own ringtone. Is it only so that we can distinguish our own phone from others or is it because ²*each/a large number of/both* time our phone rings we want to be able to say, 'Listen to that. That's me!'? Maybe ³*either/both/each* reasons are true. Here is a quick guide to ⁴*some/few/a little* typical ringtones and what they say about their users.

If your ringtone is ⁵*either/both/neither* a hip hop tune or a current hit, then you are young at heart but not particularly original.

⁶*Any/All/Either* classic rock tune means you're probably over thirty but you know you're still cool.

⁷*Not much/A few/Very few* people think annoying animal noises are as funny as the phones' owners obviously do. So ⁸*no/none/neither* points for maturity there.

You download a new one every month? You must be a teenager or you have ⁹*plenty of/a large number of/ hardly any* time and money.

You never change it? Either you're too lazy or you don't know how. ¹⁰*Neither/Both/Any* is an acceptable reason!

B Complete sentences 1–10 with a quantifier from the box.

| quite a few   a few   very few   a little   very little |
| other   another   any (x2)   either |

1 Everyone wanted to get home and so there were _____ questions at the end of the lecture.
2 I'm afraid I've spilt _____ wine on the carpet.
3 _____ of the students (four of us to be exact) have signed your petition.
4 I've watched _____ basketball games, probably twenty or thirty, but I've never seen such an exciting match.
5 Carla couldn't afford a taxi because she had _____ money left.
6 You can click on _____ 'save' or 'save as' and then give the document a name.
7 Are you having _____ other problems with the photocopier?
8 I like _____ music by Jade. She's great.
9 One car isn't enough. We need _____ car.
10 I don't care what _____ people think.

7.2 **A** Read the questions then complete the reported speech below.

1 Where have you been all day?
2 What were you watching on TV last night?
3 Have you washed your hands for dinner?
4 Have you got any homework for tomorrow?
5 Are you going to help me with the housework this weekend?

My mother used to ask me questions at the strangest times:
- When I came home from school she wanted to know ¹___*where I ...*___.
- The morning after we'd spent the evening watching TV together, she asked me ²_____.
- At 10 in the morning, she used to ask ³_____.
- In the middle of the summer holiday, she asked ⁴_____.
- When she knew I was going on a weekend camping trip with friends, she asked ⁵_____.

B Find and correct ten mistakes with reported speech in the story.

WEDNESDAY, FEBRUARY 23

My first (and most embarrassing) job interview
I was eighteen when I went for my first job interview, at a photo laboratory. The manager asked me take a seat and then asked what's my name and I was so nervous that I told him I don't understand the question. Then he wanted to know do I have any plant experience; I told that I had done some work in my grandmother's garden. He laughed and said that by 'plant' he had meant 'factory', not trees and flowers. I felt terribly embarrassed and simply told him that I have never worked in a factory. He had my file of photos and he asked that I talked about them. I was so nervous that I dropped them all on the floor! Then he asked me if I have any referees; I thought he meant the kind of referees they have in a football match, so I told him that I didn't play team sports but that I had been doing long-distance running for years. I was sure that I'd messed up the interview, but then he enquired when I can start! He wanted me that I start the following Monday!

Posted by Online Blog at 8:54PM

7.3 **A** Make the soap opera script more dramatic by using the words in brackets. Make any other changes necessary.

A: What's the matter? You look terrible. (on earth)
B: I've just seen Marco with Claudia. I'm furious, I can hardly speak. (so)
A: That's crazy. I'm sure there's a mistake. Why don't you call him? (totally)
B: I'm not going to phone him. (there's no way)
A: But Marco's a great guy and you're good together. (such, so)
B: Well, you can be sure that Claudia's going to regret it. (really)
A: I hope you're not going to do anything stupid. (do)
B: You told me to fight for him. I'm just following your advice. (the one)

GRAMMAR

8.1 past and mixed conditionals

hypothetical past conditional (third conditional)

conditional clause	result clause
If + past perfect	would/might/could + have + past participle
If + past perfect continuous	

Use this to talk about a hypothetical situation and result in the past. The situation cannot be changed.

*If Leon **had known** about the problem, he **would have helped**.*
*If you **hadn't overslept**, we **wouldn't have been** late.*

For a longer action, use the past perfect continuous.

*If I **hadn't been sitting** there, we **wouldn't have met**.*

It is common to use only one clause of the full conditional.

*Why didn't you tell me you wanted some grapes? I **could have bought** you some.*
I'm surprised Paul didn't tell her what he thought.
*I **would have said** something.*
*A: **Would you have done** it?   B: Yes, if **I'd noticed** in time.*

mixed conditional

conditional clause	result clause
If + past perfect	would/might/could + infinitive

Use this to talk about a hypothetical condition in the past with a result in the present.

*If she **hadn't missed** her plane, she**'d be** in Mexico now.*
*If **I'd been** successful in the exam, I **might have** a better job now.*

clause order

It is possible to change the order of the clauses. Note the non-use of the comma.

*You **would have known** about the meeting if you**'d checked** your emails.*
*You **wouldn't need** a visa to work in Australia if you**'d been born** there.*

8.2 -ing form and infinitive

Use an infinitive + *to*:	Examples
after these verbs: *afford, agree, arrange, decide, expect, hope, intend, learn, manage, need, offer, plan, pretend, promise, refuse, seem, tend, threaten, want*	We hope to start the meeting at 9. They promised to be here early.
after these verbs with an object: *ask, advise, expect, help*, invite, persuade, remind, require, teach, want*	Will wants me to go to the party with him.
After semi-fixed phrases: *be good/ lucky/happy/necessary/the first, have the chance/opportunity/time, somewhere/something/nowhere/ nothing*	She was lucky to get the job. There's nowhere to go and nothing to do.
to express purpose	I'm going there to see Tom.

-ing form	Examples
as a subject or object, i.e. as a noun.	Doing is better than thinking.
after prepositions (often part of a fixed phrase): *look forward to, be used to, be accustomed to, be keen on, instead of*	I'm not used to getting up early. I'm looking forward to sleeping late this weekend.
after these verbs: *avoid, come, consider, discuss, deny, enjoy, go, hate, involve, keep, like, love, mind, miss, practise, suggest*	Dave came fishing with me. I keep getting headaches. What do you suggest doing?
after certain phrases: *can't bear/ stand, it's not worth, it's no use, have trouble*	We're having trouble finding a hotel.

Use an infinitive:	Examples
after modal verbs	They might be late.
after *had better, would rather*	You'd better take an umbrella – it looks like rain.
after these verbs with an object: *let, make, help**	Our supervisor let us go early today.

*help can be used either with or without *to*.
*Can you help me **(to) lift** this?*

8.3 handling an awkward situation

preparing the listener	
There's something	I've been meaning to talk to you about. I'd like to talk to you about.

giving the message
I hope you don't take this the wrong way, but …
I don't want you to get the wrong idea, but …
It's just that, (you know you borrowed/you said you'd … etc.)

suggesting a solution
I have a suggestion/an idea.
I'd feel better if …

getting the other person's point of view
Do you see where I'm coming from?
How does that sound?
How would you feel about that?
Do you know what I mean?

PRACTICE

8.1

A Choose the correct sentence ending.

1 If the builders had begun the job two weeks ago,
   a) they might have finished it by now.
   b) they might finish it by now.

2 If Chun had started the race better,
   a) she could win the gold medal.
   b) she could have won the gold medal.

3 We wouldn't be lost
   a) if you hadn't given me the wrong directions.
   b) if you gave me the wrong directions.

4 If Marco hadn't ignored my advice,
   a) he wouldn't be in this mess now.
   b) he couldn't have been in this mess now.

5 I would have noticed the hole in the ground
   a) if I hadn't thought about something else.
   b) if I hadn't been thinking about something else.

B Join the sentences using a past or mixed conditional form and the words in brackets. In some cases both forms are possible.

1 Beth didn't study. She didn't pass the exam. (could)
   If Beth had studied, she could have passed the exam.

2 You didn't invite me to the party. That's why I didn't come. (would)

3 Ludmila lost all her money on the stock market. That's why she's not rich now. (would)

4 Greg wasn't travelling fast. That's probably why he didn't hit the motorcyclist. (might)

5 They stopped the fire. That's probably why it didn't destroy most of the building. (could)

6 The plant died because you didn't water it. (would not)

7 Mei-li was able to afford a new car because she had just won some money. (could not)

8 We were working together in Tokyo and now we're married. (would not)

8.2

A Find and correct the mistakes in the sentences. Do not change the underlined phrase.

1 It's no use to explain – you never listen anyway.
   It's no use explaining – you never listen anyway.

2 There's no point in go to bed now – we have to get up in an hour.

3 Do you expect that I know all the answers?

4 Listen to your MP3 player during class is rude.

5 My parents never let me to stay out past 8 o'clock.

6 We all look forward to see you in person.

7 You'd better to get ready – the taxi's arriving in ten minutes.

8 The trip was a good opportunity practising speaking English.

9 They're used to speak English with each other even though they're both Japanese.

10 I phoned the station for asking about departure times.

B Use the correct form of the verbs in the box to rewrite the sentences so that they mean the same.

avoid	consider	expect	keep	manage
remind	teach			

1 Why don't you become a doctor?
   Have _____.

2 I've passed my driving test – after three tries!
   I've _____.

3 I can type without looking. I learnt that from my mother.
   My mother _____.

4 We didn't talk to each other all through the party.
   We _____.

5 Jorge thinks that he'll finish the painting by the end of the week.
   Jorge _____.

6 My computer freezes whenever I hit the delete button.
   My computer _____.

7 Don't let me forget to lock the door, Jan.
   Could you _____?

8.3

A Complete the conversation with phrases a)–f). There is one phrase you do not need.

A: Max, ¹_____.
B: Sure, go ahead.
A: Look, ²_____ …
B: That sounds bad …
A: ³_____ you know how you always open the window when you come into the office? Well, it's often too cold for me.
B: Oh, right. I find it too stuffy.
A: It's a bit annoying because you don't ever ask us. ⁴_____?
B: Fair enough. Look, I'll make sure I check first. ⁵_____?
A: Good. I'd really appreciate that.

a) How does that sound
b) It's just that
c) there's something I've been meaning to talk to you about
d) I'm sure we can sort it out
e) Do you see where I'm coming from
f) I don't want you to get the wrong idea, but

GRAMMAR

9.1 -ing form and infinitive

	+ infinitive with *to*	+ -ing form
remember forget	for things you plan, want or have the responsibility to do *He remembered to turn off the lights.*	have a memory of an earlier action *I'll never forget visiting Paris.*
try	attempt to do something difficult *Angus tried to change his ticket but it was impossible.*	experiment to see if something will work *Try clicking on OK in the box.*
stop	stop one action in order to do another (infinitive of purpose) *We stopped to have some lunch.*	finish an action or activity *My father stopped driving when he was eighty.*
go on	for a change of activity *She started by defining obesity and went on to talk about its causes.*	continue *Joe went on working although he wasn't well.*
regret	be sorry about something you are about to say *BA regrets to announce a delay of flight BA5276.*	be sorry about something you did before *We regretted going to the party. It was awful.*

Verbs followed by the -ing form or infinitive with *to* with no difference in meaning

These include: *like, love, hate, prefer, can't stand, can't bear, start, begin*
I hate writing/to write by hand.
I much prefer using/to use a computer.

In American English, the infinitive with *to* is often preferred. In British English, this is often used to talk about choices and habits.
I like to go to the dentist twice a year.
I hate to interrupt, but we have to go.

If the verb after *prefer* is in the negative, use the infinitive with *to*.
I prefer not to write by hand.

When we use the verbs *begin*, *continue* and *start* in continuous forms we usually use the infinitive with *to*.
They're beginning to annoy me.
NOT ~~They're beginning annoying me.~~

9.2 past modals of deduction

Use modal verb + *have* + past participle to make deductions or guesses about past actions or states.
You could have left it in the café.

Use modal verb + *have* + *been* + -ing form to make deductions about continuous actions or states.
She must have been feeling ill.

Use modal verb + *have* + *been* + past participle for deductions using the passive.
It can't have been stolen from your bag.

must have	you are almost certain that something is true, based on the evidence	*I must have deleted the email. I can't find it anywhere.*
might/ could/ may have	you think it is possible that something is true, based on the evidence	*The plane could have been delayed by the weather. There's a bad storm at sea.*
couldn't/ can't have	you are almost certain something is not true or is impossible, based on the evidence	*It can't have been the waitress. She wasn't in the room when the bag was stolen.*

Note: *have* + past participle (the perfect infinitive) is also used with other modals: *should have (been)* and *would have (been)*.

9.3 reporting an incident

referring to time	
Before/As soon as/ When	I realised what had happened/ was happening …
It was only (a minute/much) later	(that) I realised/remembered …
It all happened	so quickly/fast/slowly.

describing impressions of a person or thing	
He reminded me of	Tom Cruise.
He looked/seemed	as if he was a student. like a student. about 30/very strong.

other phrases for reporting	
It never occurred to me It didn't cross my mind	(that) he was a thief.
My mind/I	went blank.
I didn't catch	the car number plate. what he said.

PRACTICE

9.1 **A** Match the sentence halves.

1 I tried drinking the medicine   *b*
2 I tried to drink the medicine
   a) but I couldn't – it was too disgusting.
   b) but it didn't help.

3 He stopped to smoke
4 He stopped smoking
   a) a cigarette before continuing.
   b) because he wanted to get fitter.

5 Julia remembers to text me
6 Julia remembers texting me
   a) whenever she needs a lift from the station.
   b) but I didn't get any messages from her.

7 Xavier went on to perform
8 Xavier went on performing
   a) even though audiences became smaller and smaller.
   b) in all of the best opera houses in the world.

9 We regret saying
10 We regret to say
   a) that the car won't be ready till Monday.
   b) that the Games would be a failure.

B Underline the correct alternative. Sometimes both are possible.

Most people prefer not ¹*getting/to get* involved in a crime investigation, according to Detective Jaime Lopez. 'I'll give you an example,' said Lopez. 'Last week we were just starting ²*investigating/to investigate* a car theft that had happened in broad daylight in the city centre, and we realised that our biggest challenge might be to find someone who remembered ³*seeing/to see* anything at all. We estimate that twenty or thirty people witnessed the crime but no one tried ⁴*intervening/to intervene* and most people went on ⁵*doing/to do* what they were doing. Interestingly, one tourist stopped ⁶*taking/to take* pictures of the theft in process but then continued sightseeing. He only came forward three days after the incident. "Sorry, I forgot ⁷*telling/to tell* you that I have some pictures of the crime," he said, but he didn't seem genuinely to regret ⁸*not coming forward/to not come forward* earlier. We tried ⁹*identifying/to identify* the thief from the tourist's photograph but it wasn't clear enough.' We asked Lopez how he can bear ¹⁰*doing/to do* such a frustrating job. 'I like ¹¹*helping/to help* people. I love this city. I never stop ¹²*being/to be* glad I live here.'

9.2 **A** Rewrite the underlined sentence with *must/might/ may/could/can't/couldn't have*.

1 <u>Perhaps Jenna phoned while we were out.</u> Let me check on the answerphone.
Jenna might have phoned while we were out.

2 Knock louder. You know he's a bit deaf. <u>I'm sure he didn't hear you.</u>

3 I locked the door. I'm certain. <u>Maybe the thieves got in through the window.</u>

4 I can't find the final version of the report in my computer. <u>I realised it was impossible that I saved the document.</u>

5 Ooh, that was a bad knock to your head. <u>I'm certain it hurt a lot.</u>

6 I don't know why Wanda was late for the meeting. <u>Maybe her plane was delayed.</u>

7 <u>I'm sure I've made a mistake.</u> The date looks wrong.

8 Paola should have won the race. <u>It's impossible that she was trying hard enough.</u>

B Complete the conversations with the correct form of a verb from the box and a modal of deduction.

look   tell   think   cost   work   switch off

1 A: Look at her necklace. Are those real diamonds?
  B: Yes. It _____ a fortune!

2 A: I tried phoning Mike four times but he didn't answer.
  B: He _____ his phone or maybe he left it at home.

3 A: Why was Danielle in the office at midnight?
  B: She _____ late. She had a big meeting the next day.

4 A: I'm sure Len told me you were a doctor.
  B: He _____ of my sister, Rachel, or maybe he confused me with someone else.

5 A: I've lost my boarding card. It's not in my bag!
  B: You _____ properly. I saw you put it there just now.

6 A: Do you think Yves knows he didn't get the promotion?
  B: I suppose he _____ by the boss but I doubt it.

9.3 **A** Correct each of B's sentences by adding a word from the box.

looked   realised   crossed   occurred   if   strange

A: Why didn't you phone us when you first saw the man behaving strangely?

B: ¹It never my mind until I saw the picture on *Crimebeat* on TV.

A: And when you saw *Crimebeat* … ?

B: ²It to me then that I should contact you.

A: We appreciate that. Tell me what happened.

B: ³I saw him near the factory. He looked as he was taking photos of the building.

A: Do you remember anything else?

B: ⁴When he saw me, he left quickly and he guilty.

A: Why didn't you call someone right away?

B: ⁵It was only later that I that there was something strange about how he left.

A: Maybe he'd finished?

B: ⁶I don't know. It just seemed quite but then I didn't think any more about it till I saw the programme.

GRAMMAR

10.1 relative clauses

defining relative clauses
*   give essential information about a noun.
    *That guy is the actor **who is going to play the president**.*
    Don't use commas before or after the clause.
*   can use *that* instead of *who* or *which*.
    *Ken's just seen a woman ~~who~~ **that** he went to university with.*
*   can omit the relative pronoun/adverb when it is the object of the relative clause.
    Ken's just seen a woman (who) he went to university with.
    He is the subject of the relative clause, *who* is the object, so we can omit *who*.

pronouns and adverbs in relative clauses
Use the relative pronouns *who/that* (people), *which/that* (things), *whose* (possession) and the relative adverbs *when* (time) and *where* (place).
*I remember the time **when** you were just a little girl.*
Whose can be used to refer to cities, countries and other nouns which suggest a group of people. It is rarely used with things.
*It's a city **whose** inhabitants always seem to be upbeat.*
Omit words which have been replaced by the relative pronoun.
NOT *She's someone **who** I know ~~her~~ well.*

non-defining relative clauses
*   give additional, non-essential information.
    *That's Sam, **who is going to play the president**.*
*   use commas to separate this clause from the rest of the sentence.
*   cannot use *that* instead of *who* or *which*.
    *The film, **which** won the Oscar last year, was made in India.*
    NOT ~~The film, that won the Oscar last year, was made in India.~~
*   cannot omit the relative pronouns/adverbs.
    *Gwen, **who** I'm going to see later, is my fiancé.*
    NOT ~~Gwen, I'm going to see later, is my fiancé.~~
*   can use *which* to refer to the whole of a previous clause.
    *The plane was delayed, **which** meant we were late.*

prepositions in relative clauses
In informal spoken and written English prepositions usually come at the end of the relative clause.
*This is the book **which** she's famous **for**.*
In formal and in written English prepositions often come before the relative pronoun. Use *whom* for people.
*He is someone **with whom** I can work.*
Where can be replaced by *which ... in*, or, in more formal English *in which*.
*The room **where** she slept/**which** she slept **in**/**in which** she slept is over there.*

10.2 participle clauses

*   Use participle clauses (clauses that start with a present participle or a past participle) to vary your style or to include more information in a sentence.
*   Use them as a shorter alternative to relative clauses. In this use they are also known as 'reduced relative clauses'. Form the participle clause by omitting the relative pronoun and any auxiliary verbs.
*   Clauses beginning with a past participle have a passive meaning.
    *The children **caught in the rainstorm** came home soaked.*
    = The children who were caught ...
    *The film, **directed by Miyakazi**, won an award for animation.*
    = which was directed by Miyakazi ...

*   Clauses beginning with a present participle have an active meaning.
    *The team **playing in red** is Chile.*
    = The team that is playing in red ...
    *Do you know the man **standing in the corner**?*
    = the man who is standing ...
*   Clauses beginning with a present participle replace continuous and simple verbs in different tenses.
    *Give me a number **beginning** with three.*
    = Give me a number which begins with three.
    *Anyone **cheating** in the exam failed.*
    = Anyone who cheated in the exam failed.
    *The bus **leaving** tomorrow will stop at Lima.*
    = The bus which is leaving/leaves tomorrow ...

10.3 giving a tour

commenting on facts

As you may know,/As I'm sure you know, ...
The story goes that ...
Apparently,/Supposedly,/Interestingly, ...
Surprisingly,/Strangely,/Believe it or not, ...
It's well worth (going/seeing/a visit)

leading the way

Let's/We could	head over to	the park.
Shall we	head back to	
Why don't we	retrace our steps to	the café?

giving facts

It was	built	to celebrate ... to commemorate ... in honour of ...
	founded by/ named after	(Thomas Bodley).
	modelled on/ modelled after	(the Arc de Triomphe).
	burnt down destroyed rebuilt restored	in the 15th century. in the 1990s.

PRACTICE

10.1

A Combine the sentences using a relative clause. Omit the relative pronoun where possible. Sometimes there is more than one answer.

1 The man is marrying Suzanne. He's very lucky.
   The man _____.

2 The house burnt down yesterday. I used to live in it.
   The house _____.

3 Pablo Picasso spent his early childhood in Malaga. His father was also an artist.
   Pablo Picasso _____.

4 That was the most important moment of my life. I realised I wanted to be an actor.
   The moment _____.

5 The holiday was in Canada. I enjoyed it most.
   The holiday _____.

6 Usain Bolt is a global superstar. He was the first man to win six gold Olympic medals in sprinting.
   Usain Bolt, _____.

7 I lived with a guy when I was a student. His hobby was fixing motorbikes.
   When I was _____.

8 You should make a speech. This is that sort of occasion.
   This is _____.

B Add the missing prepositions (*for, from, in, on, to* or *with*). There is one extra preposition you do not need.

1 It was the house which I spent my childhood.

2 It was a lesson which I'll always be grateful.

3 She's definitely the woman whom he wants to spend the rest of his life.

4 The cinema I most often go is the Odeon in the town centre.

5 Funnily enough, it was the planning which we spent the most time.

6 He was an athlete whom success came as naturally as his speed.

7 He was a friend I could always depend.

8 You're the person who we always turn when a speech is needed.

10.2

A Complete the sentences with the present or past participle form of the verb in brackets.

1 A beret is a type of flat hat often _____ on one side of the head. (wear)

2 The large number of people _____ outside meant the doctor would be working late that night. (wait)

3 Items permanently _____ from your inbox can usually be found again if you know where to look. (delete)

4 I knew two people _____ in the fire. (injure)

5 Babies _____ in a bilingual household have more flexible brains. (bring up)

6 The dance _____ place tomorrow is to celebrate the end of the exams. (take)

B Combine the sentences using a participle clause and the correct punctuation. Sometimes there is more than one possibility.

1 The taxi almost drove over a man. He was lying in the street.

2 *Sunflowers* was painted by Van Gogh. It's one of the most popular paintings ever.

3 The army advanced towards the hill. It was led by Napoleon.

4 I don't know the people. They live next door to me.

5 I used to like block-busters. They involved lots of action.

6 The apartments overlook Central Park. They are the most expensive.

7 Some factories were forced to close during the recession. They still haven't reopened.

8 Many people think that the Taj Mahal is the most beautiful building in the world. It was built in the seventeenth century.

10.3

A Correct eight mistakes in A's part of the conversations.

1 **A:** So here we are at Margit Island, named from a nun whose father was once king.
   B: Wow! It's beautiful.
   A: Yeah, interesting at one time it was three islands and only used by people who had land here.

2 **A:** Supposingly these caves run for miles.
   B: What were they for?
   A: The story tells that when there was an invasion, the local people hid in these tunnels.

3 **A:** That's the Vajdahunyad Castle. It was modelled from a castle in Transylvania.
   B: And why was it built?
   A: It was built for the city's millennium exhibition in 1896, to memorise the one-thousand-year anniversary of the founding of the state.

4 **A:** Let's retrace our feet to Castle Hill.
   B: Great. We hardly spent any time there this morning.
   A: Exactly, and the museum is well worse a visit.

VOCABULARY BANK

Lesson 6.1
WORD-BUILDING: PREFIXES

1 A Find a prefix in A which means:

1 very small
2 very big
3 many
4 between
5 two
6 across

bi   multi
micro   mega
trans   inter

lingual   chip
national   media
late   wave   port
task   phone   cycle
scope   val   monthly
city   view   it
-storey   byte

B Match a prefix in A with at least three endings in B.

C Complete the sentences with the correct form of a word formed from a prefix in A and an ending in B.

1 I left my car in one of those huge _____ car parks and now I can't find it.
2 It's a long opera but there are two _____. We can take a break and have a coffee then.
3 I've never really been to Hong Kong, only in the airport when I was in _____ on my way to Beijing.
4 The crowd was so noisy, I had to use a _____ to make my voice loud enough.
5 He didn't get the job because he was late for the _____.
6 No, it's too small. You can only see it under a _____.
7 Our newsletter only goes out _____. It's January now, so the next one is in March.
8 People who grow up in a _____ environment end up understanding three or more languages.

Lesson 6.2   TIME IDIOMS

2 A Match the phrases and idioms in bold with pictures A–I.

1 Your food will be here **in no time**.   _c_
2 Sorry, I'll have to **cut this short**. _____
3 He's **dragging his heels** over the decorating. _____
4 I was **making up for lost time** – you see I overslept. _____
5 I've told you **time after time** to take your shoes off! _____
6 She got home **in the nick of time**. _____
7 I'm just **killing an hour or two** before my interview. _____
8 Please **take your time**. _____
9 The train should be here **any time now**. _____

B Match meanings a)–i) to the phrases and idioms.

a) to spend time doing something unimportant while you are waiting for something else to happen
b) very soon
c) very quickly
d) to delay doing something
e) to do something without hurrying
f) again and again
g) to stop doing something earlier than you had planned
h) at the last moment before it is too late to do something
i) to do something quickly because you started late or worked too slowly

Lesson 7.1 MULTI-WORD VERBS

1 A Look at the sentence pairs. How are the meanings of the multi-word verbs in bold different?

1 Did your parents **bring** you **up** as a Buddhist?

2 Oh, here's Edith now. Just don't **bring up** anything about her divorce.

3 Anna keeps **putting off** the meeting. I don't think we'll ever get a chance to discuss things.

4 Stop talking about your illnesses. You're **putting** me **off** my food!

5 Why did they **turn** Neil **down** for the job?

6 Could you **turn** the cooker **down** – the sauce in the pan is going to burn.

7 My car's in the garage. It **broke down** on the way to work today.

8 Negotiations between the two corporations have **broken down**, but they may restart next month.

9 The company **took on** ten school-leavers last month.

10 After Brazil won the semi-finals, they **took on** the favourites, Spain.

11 He **pulled out** without looking and hit another car.

12 Both countries have **pulled out** of the talks, so there won't be any agreement.

B Complete the table with the multi-word verbs from Exercise 1A.

a		hire compete against
b		say no lower the level
c		end one's involvement, or quit drive onto a road from another road
d		make sb dislike sth postpone
e		raise start to talk about
f		fail or end unsuccessfully stop working, usually for a machine

Lesson 7.3 PARTS OF A NEWS WEBSITE

2 Match 1–10 to the parts of a news website.

1 breaking news
2 lead story
3 headlines
4 news feed
5 forum link
6 weather forecast
7 video link
8 menu bar
9 navigation buttons
10 popup ad

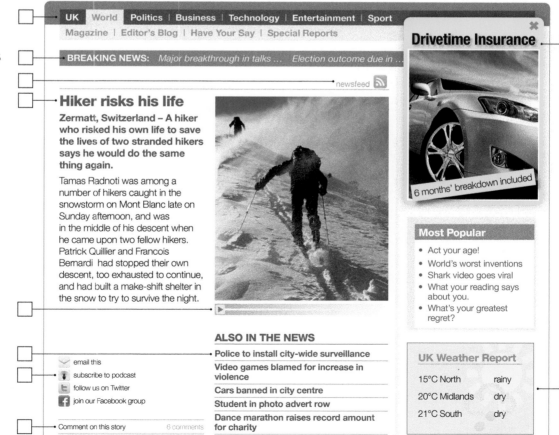

UK | World | Politics | Business | Technology | Entertainment | Sport

Magazine | Editor's Blog | Have Your Say | Special Reports

BREAKING NEWS: *Major breakthrough in talks ... Election outcome due in ...*

newsfeed

Hiker risks his life

Zermatt, Switzerland – A hiker who risked his own life to save the lives of two stranded hikers says he would do the same thing again.

Tamas Radnoti was among a number of hikers caught in the snowstorm on Mont Blanc late on Sunday afternoon, and was in the middle of his descent when he came upon two fellow hikers. Patrick Quillier and Francois Bernardi had stopped their own descent, too exhausted to continue, and had built a make-shift shelter in the snow to try to survive the night.

email this
subscribe to podcast
follow us on Twitter
join our Facebook group

Comment on this story   6 comments

Drivetime Insurance

6 months' breakdown included

Most Popular

- Act your age!
- World's worst inventions
- Shark video goes viral
- What your reading says about you.
- What's your greatest regret?

ALSO IN THE NEWS

Police to install city-wide surveillance

Video games blamed for increase in violence

Cars banned in city centre

Student in photo advert row

Dance marathon raises record amount for charity

UK Weather Report

15°C North   rainy

20°C Midlands   dry

21°C South   dry

VOCABULARY BANK

Lesson 8.1 COMPOUND ADJECTIVES FOR DESCRIBING PEOPLE

1 A Look at the picture and complete the compound adjectives with words from the box.

brand   broad   brown
curly   dark   high
sun   tight

B Which words or phrases can be turned into opposites by using the opposite of the first part?

curly-haired – straight-haired

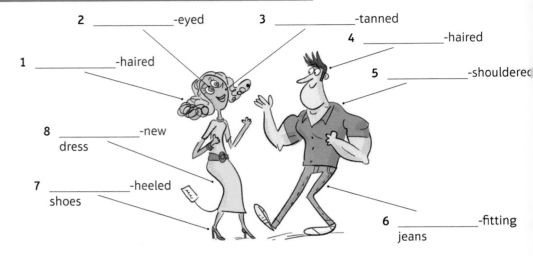

2 _____-eyed
3 _____-tanned
4 _____-haired
1 _____-haired
5 _____-shouldered
8 _____-new dress
7 _____-heeled shoes
6 _____-fitting jeans

Lesson 8.3 BEHAVIOUR IDIOMS

2 A Match pictures A–F with the idioms in the box. Two idioms are not in the pictures.

talk behind sb's back   walk all over sb
not lift a finger   be always there for sb
go out of one's way to do sth   lock horns with sb
(be) a shoulder to cry on   give sb a helping hand

B Which of the idioms in the box do you think are positive, and which are negative?

C Complete the sentences with the correct form of the idioms.

1 She loves to help out. She'll _____ anyone a _____ _____ if they need it.
2 He often sits and watches me clean and doesn't _____ _____ _____ to help.
3 When I'm really upset and need a _____ _____ _____ _____, I always turn to Martin.
4 I don't trust her, she's such a gossip. She's always _____ _____ my _____.
5 He argues about everything. In fact he'll _____ _____ _____ you on just about any topic.
6 She's the best friend I can imagine. She _____ _____ _____ for me, through good times and bad.
7 He's so kind and generous. He'll always _____ _____ _____ his _____ to help you.
8 Don't just do everything he wants. He's very selfish. Don't let him _____ _____ _____ you.

D Match meanings 1–8 to the idioms in Exercise 2A.

1 be available whenever somebody needs you
2 do something to help even though it's not convenient for you
3 be in conflict with somebody
4 do something to help somebody
5 give somebody sympathy when they're upset
6 say something (usually bad) about somebody when they're not listening
7 treat someone very badly
8 do absolutely nothing to help

Lesson 9.1 DEPENDENT PREPOSITIONS

1 Complete the headlines with a dependent preposition.

1 **Innocent man mistaken _____ gang leader**

2 **Woman jailed for hiding robbers _____ police**

3 *Couple punished _____ balloon hoax*

4 **Mugger caught after boasting _____ crimes in local bar**

5 **Jailed criminal prohibited _____ selling his story**

6 **Politician condemned _____ involvement in banking scandal**

7 Murderess given strong sentence for joking _____ crime

8 **Local teacher fired for participating _____ protest march**

9 **College president conceals financial woes _____ board of trustees**

10 Mother fined _____ leaving baby unattended in car

Lesson 9.3 CARS AND ACCIDENTS

2 Match the car parts 1–12 to A–L in the picture.

1 boot _J_
2 bonnet
3 number plate
4 indicator
5 wing
6 wing mirror
7 tail light
8 windscreen
9 tyre
10 windscreen wiper
11 sun roof
12 steering wheel

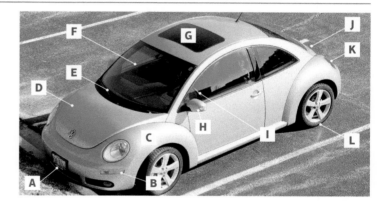

3 Complete the sentences with the verbs and verb phrases in the box in the past simple.

| skid   collide with   pull out   overtake   drive the wrong way   swerve   exceed the speed limit   scratch |

The car _____ on the ice.

She _____ to avoid hitting the dog.

She increased her speed and _____ the blue car.

He _____. He was going at 100 kph.

She _____ the side of the car by parking too near a wall.

He was driving too fast in a narrow street and _____ another car.

A car _____ in front of him and he almost crashed into it.

He _____ down the motorway.

VOCABULARY BANK

Lesson 10.2 MUSIC

1 A Match the instruments 1–12 with the photos.

1 acoustic guitar
2 drums
3 bass guitar
4 violin/fiddle (informal)
5 cello
6 grand piano
7 trumpet
8 trombone
9 flute
10 clarinet
11 saxophone
12 harp

B Can you play any of the instruments above? Which instrument would you most like to learn?

2 Match the phrases and idioms in bold with meanings a)–h).

1 There goes Jim again, saying how great he is, **blowing his own trumpet**.
2 Clara began **fiddling with** her necklace. I could see that she was worried.
3 We need to **drum up** some new business or we'll have to close down.
4 I'm tired of **playing second fiddle**.
5 Interesting how Larry **changed his tune** after he found out it was his own assistant who stole the money.
6 I know, it looks like an expensive car but I got it **for a song**.
7 The boss wants to see me about my mistakes on the contract. It's time for me to go in and **face the music**.
8 Her name **rings a bell** – maybe I've met her before.

a) take a less important role
b) remind sb of sth, sound familiar
c) talk positively about oneself
d) touch or play with something in a restless or nervous way
e) get (support or attention) through making a lot of effort
f) accept responsibility for mistakes
g) suddenly take a different perspective
h) very cheaply

Lesson 10.2 TWO-PART PHRASES

3 A Complete the sentences with the words in the box.

take   death   leave   later   swim   another   miss   nothing

1 It's only a question of time, and **sooner or** _____ you'll find a new job.
2 That's the highest salary we can pay you. We can't go higher, so **take it or** _____ it.
3 You've finished the training, and now you have to go out and do the job. It's **sink or** _____.
4 The shop is about twenty kilometres from here, **give or** _____ a kilometre.
5 It was **all or** _____ – she either had to get in the car with him or lose him forever.
6 This is the biggest choice of my life – it's a **life or** _____ decision.
7 Mark took a **hit or** _____ approach to finding a girlfriend. He simply asked every girl he saw out on a date.
8 I know, we're lost, but **one way or** _____ we'll find our way back.

B Match meanings a)–h) with the two-part phrases in Exercise 3A.

a) the offer won't change
b) risking everything
c) to within (a small amount)
d) unplanned/disorganised
e) eventually
f) somehow
g) fail or succeed
h) extremely important

Lesson 7.3

7 **B** Student A

The top five most dangerous animals

1 mosquito 2 Asian cobra 3 Australian box jellyfish
4 great white shark 5 African lion

Lesson 10.2

8 **A** Student B

T **through and through** completely: *a typical Englishman through and through*

O **on and on** used to say that someone continues to do something, or that something continues to happen: *He talked on and on about his job.*

R **rough and ready** (= not perfect, but good enough to use)

N **(every) now and then/now and again** sometimes: *He sees her every now and then at college.*

U **ups and downs** n [plural] the good and bad things that happen in life, business, etc: *Every marriage has its ups and downs.*

Lesson 10.5

3 **c**

1 Sydney Opera House
2 Apple Inc.
3 squash
4 Napoleon Bonaparte
5 Oscar
6 the Inuit
7 sushi (makizushi)
8 *Hamlet*

Lesson 6.2

7 **c**

Key
a) = 3 points
b) = 2 points
c) = 1 point

12–15: You are amazingly optimistic! On the one hand, your positive attitude can make people around you feel good. On the other hand, sometimes people may find your constant cheerfulness slightly irritating.

8–11: You are calm and level-headed and can always see both sides of a situation. This means you don't have great highs and lows but can also mean you miss out on some of the drama of life.

5–7: You're not always easy to be with, usually seeing the negative side of things. However, this can be extremely useful in some situations because you will tend to be more cautious and see what could go wrong with any plans or projects.

Lesson 6.3

7 **B** Student A

1 You are going to take part in a radio phone-in, and you are the DJ. Ask Student B to tell you about their situation. Ask for clarification to check you understand. Then invite Student C to give their opinion. Encourage B and C to exchange their points of view.

2 Now change roles. You are a caller. Give your opinion when the DJ asks you.

3 Now change roles. You are a different caller. Explain your situation to the DJ:

A well-known social networking site has a minimum age of thirteen. Your daughter is thirteen next week and she says some of her friends' parents have allowed their children to join. You think she's too young.

Lesson 9.2

7 D

Free gift wrapping

Preparation:

1 The con artist team goes to a busy shopping mall during the festival season and sets up a tent with a sign saying 'Free gift wrapping'.

2 An attractive, friendly, female con artist stands behind the counter.

3 The other two con artists are inside the tent, out of sight. They have a scale for weighing things, oranges and packing material.

The scam:

1 When a customer brings an item for wrapping, the woman passes it into the tent.

2 The two con artists there open the package, remove the item and weigh it, then put the same weight in oranges into the box with packing material and wrap it attractively.

3 They pass it back to the female colleague, who gives it to the customer. The package feels like the original and won't be opened till later!

Hire car scam

Preparation:

1 The con artist team hires an expensive car, changes the number plates and removes any evidence that it's hired.

2 The team places an advert in a newspaper or online offering the car at a very low price.

3 The team finds an empty house, breaks in and puts some toys around the rooms and driveway. This address is given when people answer the advert.

The scam:

1 An attractive female con artist poses as a young mother and greets customers as they arrive. She explains to the customers why there are no car papers. Some of the customers will offer a cash deposit.

2 At the end of the afternoon, the team clears out of the house, returns the car to the hire agency and disappears.

Lesson 6.3

7 B Student B

1 You are going to take part in a radio phone-in, and you are a caller. Explain your situation to the DJ:
Your son, who is seventeen, has started going out with a young woman who he says is the love of his life. He wants to get a tattoo linking her name and his. You're strongly against the idea.

2 Now change roles. You are the DJ. Ask Student C to tell you about their situation. Ask for clarification to check you understand. Then invite Student A to give their opinion. Encourage A and C to exchange their points of view.

3 Now change roles. You are a different caller. Give your opinion when the DJ asks you.

Lesson 7.3

7 B Student B

The top five countries with the tallest people

1 the Netherlands 2 Sweden 3 Denmark
4 Norway 5 Estonia

Lesson 9.3

8 A Student B

Lesson 10.2

1 C Student A: read the text on this page. Which four questions below does it answer?

1 How do actors cry on demand?

2 Do big stars have to audition for film roles?

3 How do singers keep their voices steady when they're dancing?

4 Why is rock music played so loud at concerts?

5 Who decides whether something is 'art' or not?

6 Why do works of art get stolen if they can't be sold without attracting attention?

7 What's the secret to making an audience laugh?

8 How does a comedian deal with hecklers?

D Read the text again. Write a maximum of five key words for each answer to help you remember the information.

E Work in pairs. Cover the text and look at your notes from Exercise 1D. Tell your partner about the answers.

POPULAR CULTURE

Want to know the best-kept secrets of popular culture? Read our Top Questions & Answers to find out.

Q:

A: Singers such as Beyoncé, whose stage show involves her dancing all over the stage, can't always deliver high-quality vocals live as it's physically extremely difficult to control the voice while jumping around. Because of this, many performers rely on a backing track to provide vocals during some songs, and whilst they may be singing live, the audience can't actually hear their voice. Some stationary performers use a backing track when they're concerned about difficult parts of the performance, for example hitting a very high note or even remembering the words to a song.

Q:

A: Every comedian has his or her own strategy for dealing with members of the audience interrupting their performance with rude comments. Strategies range from simply telling the heckler to be quiet ('Shut up!') to humiliating the heckler into silence by insulting them or someone with them such as their girlfriend. Armed with the microphone, the comedian has a great advantage over the heckler. Some comedians, known for their particularly aggressive way of handling hecklers, actually become more famous for this aspect of their act than their scripted sections.

Q:

A: There are certain ways of making it look like you're crying, such as putting glycerine in your eyes, sniffing a freshly cut onion or, on stage, concentrating on a bright point of light. Most actors use more internal techniques that exploit emotional memory. By recalling a time when they were sad or upset, an actor can often get the tears flowing. Or sometimes they'll build an association between an object – a prop they'll be handling during the scene – and that emotion, so that, when they touch the prop, they feel inclined to cry. Interestingly, most actors say it's easier to cry convincingly than to laugh convincingly.

Q:

A: This is an age-old question. The range of works and styles of painting regarded as art at different times is astonishing – from ancient Chinese ink paintings to Leonardo Da Vinci to Jackson Pollock. One argument goes that a painting is art if the painter says it is, and gives convincing reasons to support their position. Many artists would reject this idea; they don't care who regards their work as art. We'll probably never agree on who the most beautiful woman or best-looking man is, so we'll just have to enjoy exploring and sharing our notions of art and beauty without a definitive answer.

Lesson 10.2

8 A Student A

G **give and take** n [U] If there is give and take between two people, each person agrees to do some of the things that the other person wants: *In any relationship there has to be some give and take.*

B **be sick and tired of sb/sth** to be annoyed and bored with a person or situation: *I'm sick and tired of waiting.*

P **peace and quiet** When everything is quiet and calm: *All I want is some peace and quiet.*

L **leaps and bounds** *He improved in leaps and bounds* (= very much, very quickly).

T **the pros and cons (of sth)** the advantages and disadvantages of something

Lesson 7.3

7 B Student C

The top five cities for art lovers

1 Berlin   2 Chicago   3 Florence

4 London   5 New York

Lesson 9.2

7 A Student A: imagine the following situation happened to you. Add some details about the place, time, the amount of money of the deposit, and your feelings. Prepare to tell Student B.

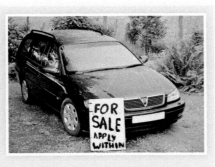

I went round to a house to look at a car. I'd seen the advert earlier. There were kids' toys in the driveway by the car. A young woman, the kids' mother I guessed, showed me round the car – it was a fantastic bargain and I wanted to buy it. She couldn't show me the car papers because her husband had just taken them to pay the car tax. She told me that she'd got lots of other interested people coming round later so I gave her a deposit and she said I could pick up the car at six. At six o'clock, I found eight other people outside the house, no car and no one at home.

B Listen to Student B's situation and discuss his/her questions.

C Tell Student B the situation and discuss these questions.
1 Who was the woman?
2 How did she trick people into thinking she was a mother?
3 Who did the car belong to?
4 Who were the other eight people?
5 How do you think the scam was done?

D Turn to page 144 to see if your ideas were right.

Lesson 7.3

7 B Student D
The top five friendliest countries
1 Ireland 2 the USA 3 Malawi 4 Fiji 5 Thailand

Lesson 6.3

7 B Student C
1 You are going to take part in a radio phone-in, and you are a caller. Give your opinion when the DJ asks you.
2 Now change roles. You are a different caller. Explain your situation to the DJ:
   Your eighteen-year-old son has just passed his driving test. He wants to borrow your car so that he can drive his friends around. He says that his other friends' parents let them borrow their cars. You think he's not ready yet.
3 Now change roles. You are the DJ. Ask Student A to tell you about their situation. Ask for clarification to check you understand. Then invite Student B to give their opinion. Encourage A and B to exchange their points of view.

Lesson 9.3

8 A Student A

Lesson 9.5

4 B
1 The man always checked the post box before the postman came. His wife took the letters out when they arrived.
2 A record company was making a recording of the performance and had asked the audience not to applaud, so that the recording would be clean.

AUDIO SCRIPTS

OK … so … Dear the future me, I hope this letter has found its way to you/me. As I write this, I am sixteen in year eleven; and as I read it, I am twenty. Wow! I will have changed so much. I can only guess what I will be like at twenty. I envisage myself at Oxford Uni, sitting … oh, this is embarrassing … sitting under a tree by the river in the college grounds. I think I'll be wearing something floaty and a bit indie, but I bet when I get this, it'll be raining.

I know, I'm a romantic. I hope that hasn't changed. My plans for myself in the following years are to find a man, someone good-looking, romantic and intelligent who shares my interests. Either way, I hope I'll have someone. I don't remember this … and then I think I'll have three children with long, brown hair and green eyes.

Well, I'll stop now even though I want to write everything I can down, but I'm running out of time. I hope I'm happy, and I hope this letter makes me feel good about who I was, or am, as I write this. Keep smiling, and while I can't really say bye, but good luck for the future and keep dreaming. Don't change too much, and be happy with who you are – I like who I am now more than any other time.

Love, Laura.

It all seems really shallow looking back and reading what I thought I'd be doing or hoped I'd be doing. I think my sixteen-year-old self might have been disappointed with where I am, but because I as my twenty-year-old self have sort of grown up and matured, I'm absolutely ecstatic with where I am, and it doesn't have to be this perfect sitting-by-a-lake kind of image.

P = Presenter   E = Ed   J = Julia   D = Dan
Z = Zara

P: And up next, it's time for 'Just tell me I'm wrong.' Today's topic: how young is too young or, perhaps more accurately, how old is old enough? We've received hundreds of calls, emails and text messages about the right age for a child to do all sorts of things like have a smartphone. In fact our first caller asks about just that. His name is Ed. Go ahead, Ed. You're on.
E: Hi. My situation is that my eight-year-old kept asking for a smartphone, and eventually we bought her one a few months ago. Then, last week, I got a bill for over £200! I knew something like this would happen.
P: So basically you think she's too young for a phone?
E: Yeah, yeah, that's right.
P: Surely it's up to the parents to set guidelines.
E: So what you're saying is I should give her some rules?

P: Exactly. Right from the beginning. OK, thanks, Ed. Next caller is Julia. What's your question, Julia?
J: My question is about social networking sites. I don't let my daughter use them. She's only ten and I'm worried about online bullying.
P: So in other words, you're worried about kids being horrible to other kids.
J: Yeah. You hear so much about it nowadays.
P: That's a very good point. Online bullying is a serious problem … but isn't it better to talk it over with her? I'm sure they have lessons at school about how to stay safe online. She has to learn some time.
J: So what you mean is I'm being overprotective?
P: To be honest, yes. And if you try and stop her, she'll only find a way to go onto a social networking site in secret. And if she ends up in a bullying situation and you haven't prepared her, that could be much worse.
J: Oh dear … I'm sure you're right but it's not easy being a parent nowadays.
P: I agree. Thanks for your question, Julia. Let's go to our next caller. Dan, you're on.
D: Hi, my question's also about technology.
P: It seems like that's everyone's main worry. Anyway, go ahead Dan.
D: Well, my son, Seth, he's twelve and, up till recently he was a normal twelve-year-old, you know, he used to go out with his friends, play football with me, you know … we had a great relationship.
P: So, Dan, basically I'm guessing he doesn't want to spend so much time with you now and you feel …
D: Oh no, it's not that. It's just that he spends all his time on the computer now.
P: Surely that's just normal nowadays.
D: It's hard to say. Sometimes at the weekend he spends all day in his bedroom on social networking sites or playing video games. I don't think it's right. I mean for one thing, he never gets any exercise.
P: Don't you think it's just a stage he's going through? I used to spend hours in my bedroom listening to music when I was that age.
D: So what you mean is I should just relax and let him get on with it?
P: Yeah, he'll grow out of it. And you can't force him to go and play football if he doesn't want to.
D: I guess not. Thanks.
P: OK, our next caller is Zara. You're on.
Z: Um, I was wondering how you would deal with a thirteen-year-old wanting to get pierced ears?
P: Thirteen years old? Doesn't she simply want to be like her friends? I imagine a lot of them have pierced ears.
Z: Well … that's it. I'm not talking about a she.
P: Oh, in other words you're upset because your thirteen-year-old son wants to get his ears pierced.
Z: That's right.
P: Ah … so it's because he's a boy rather than his age?
Z: I suppose so.
P: Well, does he have friends who've got …

W = Woman   M = Man

W: I'm going to speak against the statement: 'Employers should give preference to younger applicants when hiring.' The first point I'd like to make is that selecting a person for a job on the basis of their age is unfair. It's as bad as choosing someone because of their gender or race or religion. People should be selected for a job because of their abilities and suitability and not because they are a certain age. For example, if a sixty-year-old person is able, physically and mentally, to do a job, they should be judged on the same basis as a thirty-year-old.
M: I would like to speak in favour of the statement. I would like to start off by saying that I fully support equal opportunities for people applying for a job. However, I would like to pick up on the point made by Sarah when she said 'if a person is able, physically and mentally, to do a job'. I think we need to be realistic here. As people age, this can affect their energy, their ability to react quickly and their memory. In some jobs it may be vital for people to have high levels of energy, for example in a creative industry such as advertising. Or people need to be able to react quickly, for instance if they're a lorry driver, or be able to concentrate for long periods of time if they're an airline pilot. It is simply a fact of life that, as we age, our mental and physical capabilities deteriorate and that, for certain jobs, younger people are better.

P = Presenter   H = Hoaxer

P: Welcome to *Insight*, where the topic for the day is hoaxes, specifically photo hoaxes. It was extremely difficult get someone who produces hoax photos, a hoaxer, to agree to appear on the show, and it was only on condition that we promise to keep his identity secret. So, I'd like to welcome my guest to the show.
H: Thank you.
P: For starters, can you explain why you want to remain anonymous?
H: Two reasons really. I suppose, one is mystery. What I mean is a good hoax photo is more powerful if people don't know where it came from. If people knew I'd produced the photo, the effect would be lost.
P: Fair enough. And the other reason?
H: Well, it's a fact that hoaxers often use photographs taken by someone else, and often without permission, and the original photographer could sue us.
P: So basically, you're playing it safe then.
H: Yeah, you could put it that way.
P: OK. Now I asked you before the show if you'd ever earned money for your hoax work, and you said that you often work with the police and detectives. What exactly do you do for the police?

H: Well, when a politician, for example, appears in a published photograph in any … embarrassing situation, say accepting money … sometimes the police ask me to look at it. Then, if I decide if the photograph is a hoax, they see if they can find out who did it.

P: Right. OK, well, let's look at some photographs that we found on the internet – some hoaxes; some not. Talk us through the photographs if you would.

H: So, this photo of a bike in a tree looks like a hoax simply because it's such an unusual image. Also, it looks a bit like a composite photo …

P: What's a composite photo?

H: When you combine two or more photos, that's a composite. In this case, it would be very easy to put a picture of the two halves of the bike over a photo of a tree. In fact, this would be a very easy hoax photo to put together.

P: So what you're saying is, it isn't real.

H: No, it actually is real. I wasn't sure myself, but I found out it was near Seattle, Washington. So I asked a friend who lives there, and he told me he'd seen it with his own eyes a number of years before. Apparently, there are many different legends about how it got there.

P: Well, I thought that one was definitely a hoax. Let's look at the next one. This one could be real. A man hanging on the landing gear of a jet plane is such an extraordinary sight, maybe that's why it looks a bit fake.

H: Well, even if you'd never seen such a thing, common sense would tell you that a man couldn't survive even the landing. The wind would pull him off.

P: Then it IS a hoax photo.

H: Yes, a classic composite photo. Not badly put together, though.

P: Remarkable. Now this next one could be real, sharks swimming through a flooded suburb. I remember seeing this on the internet. After one of those big hurricanes.

H: Ha, you've probably seen lots of photos like this, and maybe this exact one.

P: Why? Why's it funny?

H: I'm ninety-nine percent sure this is a hoax simply because it's a cliché – yet another photo of sharks swimming where they shouldn't be! Look on the internet and you'll find plenty of hoax photos of sharks.

P: And that's it? Is there a technical reason why you know it's a hoax?

H: Well, yes. The water next to the fins isn't right. The surface of the water would break differently if there really were sharks there. Look closely.

P: I see. You know, it seems like a lot of work. Why do people do it? It can't be for the money.

H: I dunno. I can only speak for myself and to be honest I'm thrilled when people believe one of my photos.

P: Because they want to believe it?

H: Well, yes. Maybe we all like to believe something really unusual could be true.

UNIT 7 Recording 4

Conversation 1

A: Wow!

B: What's that?

A: It's this story. Listen to this. 'A woman used a wooden soup ladle to save her husband from attack by a tiger'.

B: What? A ladle?

A: Well, her husband was being attacked by a tiger.

B: Where was this?

A: In Malaysia. Apparently, her husband had just gone into the forest. She saw the tiger attack him and grabbed the first thing she could find, which was a wooden soup ladle. And she just charged at the animal yelling at the top of her voice and bashing its head.

B: And it didn't attack her?

A: No. The amazing thing is that the tiger ran off.

B: Wow, there's no way I'd do that!

A: Not even for me?

B: Not even for you! You're the one who's always telling me to stop.

A: Stop what?

B: Stop helping people so much.

A: I didn't mean to stop helping me!

Conversation 2

A: Hey, Mike. Did you buy a lottery ticket?

B: No, why?

A: Well, you want to be careful. It says here that some store clerks are taking the winnings. You know when customers take in a winning ticket and they have to check it in the store …

B: Yeah …

A: Well, these guys have been telling customers that they didn't win and then they take the winning tickets for themselves.

B: That's so wrong! Suppose it was, like, a big amount?

A: One of the tickets was for $1,000 and the …

B: That's totally outrageous!

A: Yeah. Exactly.

B: So, how did they find it out?

A: The police did some undercover investigations at convenience stores. And … yeah, one of them was for $1,000 and the …

B: Hey, maybe we won something …

A: In your dreams. You don't buy lottery tickets anyway.

B: That's true.

A: But it's weird that the customers didn't notice, isn't it? That's more surprising than the actual theft.

B: Yeah. I do think they should do something about it.

A: Who?

B: The lottery companies.

A: They are doing something about it. They're going to install machines so you can check your own numbers.

B: That is a good idea.

Conversation 3

A: That's extraordinary!

B: What is?

A: This story about the baby in China.

B: What happened?

A: It's about a baby and apparently it climbed out onto a window ledge on the second floor. Oh there's a video … And, oh look, you can see these people underneath just holding out their arms because they know it's going to fall. And there are some people putting cardboard down to try and break the fall. Wow!

B: Let me see. Wow! Look at that man! How on earth did he catch it?

A: 'Just human instinct,' that's what one man said.

B: What a catch! That's such an amazing thing!

A: It's lucky the men noticed the baby.

B: Yeah, I suppose they saw some movement.

A: Or maybe they heard something.

B: What's that? The woman's bringing something.

A: It's hard to say but it looks like a cushion.

B: Yeah, it could be a sofa cushion.

A: I guess they thought the baby might fall on it.

B: That must be the luckiest baby alive.

A: Absolutely incredible. Let me see again.

UNIT 7 Recording 8

M = Man   W = Woman

M: Did you hear this story in the news about this guy that swapped a paper clip for a house?

W: No.

M: It sounds a bit out there but apparently what happened was he started … he was at his desk looking for a job or phoning up about jobs …

W: Yeah.

M: … and, um, he saw a paper clip on his desk, and he thought, I wonder what I can do with this paper clip – whether I can swap it for something.

W: Oh.

M: Anyway, so he got onto the internet and he made this website – I think it's called the-red-paper-clip dot com.

W: Right.

M: And he put this, this on the internet, photographs it, puts it on, and sees if anyone wants to swap something with him.

W: And did, did anything happen?

M: Yeah, so first of all, I don't remember all the details but as I recall two Vancouver women, um, took up the first challenge and they swapped the paper clip with, I think it was a pen shaped like a fish they had found …

W: Random.

M: Yeah – they had found on a camping trip, yeah random. But he meets up with all these people he doesn't just send the things. And so then from that, I believe, this guy in Seattle wanted the pen and swapped it for a doorknob. And the door knob was swapped for something to do with camping, …

W: Oh, so he kept trading up each time.

M: Yeah, he kept trading, trading up so, and then that was swapped for a beer keg I think. Apparently what happened was all these people were … the same sort of thought patterns as him and they wanted to sort of meet up and it was about a social event as well.

W: Ah.

M: Anyway, the next thing he got was a snow globe and, according to the report, it said a film director wanted it and said he'd swap it for a part in his film. And then this town decided they had this house in this town, and that they would swap the house for a part in this film.

W: No! So he went all the way from the red paper clip to getting a house.

M: … a house. And my impression was that he, he was just crazy at the beginning but he, he ended up having this – I'm not sure how good the house was but, well, yeah.

W: Well, better than a paper clip.

M: I know basically that's what happened.

W: Wow!

UNIT 8 Recording 2

P = Presenter   D = Dominic   H = Heather

P: OK, Dominic and Heather we're going to play a game

D: Oh.

H: Ahem.

P: Its, it's an experiment. Um what I'm gonna do is – hang on I'm just gonna get it out of my pocket. I'm going to give you, Dominic, £10.

D: OK, can I keep it?

P: OK – for now. And you have to decide how much you're going to offer Heather.

D: OK.

P: And if Heather accepts then you divide the money as agreed. You get some and she gets some.

D: Right.

P: But, if Heather rejects your offer and she doesn't like the way you've split the £10 …

D: Mmm.

P: … then I get the £10 back and neither of you get anything.

H: Um.

D: Ah, OK.

H: OK.

P: Could you understand?

D: Yeah, I think so.

H: Yeah.

P: Are you sure?

H: Yeah.

D: Yeah – so I basically have to choose how much money I'm going to offer Heather.

P: Yeah.

H: And then …

D: And if she's happy with it …

H: I decide if I want it or not.

P: That's right, OK?

H: OK?

D: So …

P: Right there you go.

D: Thank you, that's for me. That's a lot of money, I would quite like all of it. Uh, do I just say it now, out loud?

P: Yeah.

D: OK, uh I'm going to offer you £5.

P: Um.

H: Go on then, I'll accept that.

D: Yeah.

H: Yeah, I will yeah.

D: Great so we get a five, fiver each.

P: You do indeed and I, and I lose £10.

D: Yeah, that was worth it.

P: OK, so I mean that's really interesting. Why, why Dominic did you decide on that split?

D: Um, I guess, if I offered any less I didn't think you'd take it.

H: No.

D: So I thought this way.

P: But why, why, why would you?

D: Um, because it's, it's not fair, you know cos this isn't any more my money than it is hers really, just cos it's a game, you've given it to me.

P: Interesting.

D: Um it, it was.

P: And why, why did you accept?

H: Um, because I felt that it was equal you know an, an equal split, um, I thought it was very kind and yeah generous to give me half.

D: Uh.

P: OK and um, OK then – here's an interesting question. Heather, in your mind what would have …

H: Um …

P: been the lowest amount?

D: Ahem.

H: It act-

P: that you would have accepted?

H: It actually would have been £5 because I think any lower than that and I'd have felt sort of you know.

D: Hard done by.

P: Very interesting.

H: Hard done by, yeah, is the word, yeah.

P: Thanks guys, cheers.

UNIT 8 Recording 3

P = Presenter   D = Dominic   H = Heather

P: OK guys, uh we're gonna play another game now.

D: Um.

P: It's called the Dictator game. And, uh, I think I'm gonna be very out of pocket by the end of the day.

D: More money?

P: Yeah. Another £10 note.

H: Oh, a ten.

P: And, I'm gonna give it to you again.

D: Thank you.

P: But this time – instead of making an offer which you can, you Heather can accept or reject …

H: OK.

P: You have to accept it.

D: Ah.

P: So Dominic …

D: OK.

H: OK.

D: I have the power.

P: It's your decision. You have the power. It's your decision.

D: Um, OK so I just say it out loud?

P: Yeah.

D: Uh, the offer I'm going to give you this time is £1 and that means £9 will be for me.

P: OK.

H: Well then I accept that cos I have no choice.

D: You have no choice.

P: You have no choice. But, but the question here is how do you feel, how do you feel about that?

H: Yeah I feel a bit hard done by, to be honest. I feel a bit cheated really, um.

P: His fairness, from last time has all disappeared.

H: Yeah, mm.

D: Um I guess I gave you a pound to still show that I'm, you know, not heartless.

H: Ahem.

D: Uh, you know so, you know I want to keep all of it, but um I guess with the offer of being able to have more, without the choice.

H: Um.

D: Um, it sort of, it was easier for me, to say, I won't feel so guilty, I don't feel.

H: Yeah tempting, isn't it?

D: Feel a bit guilty now, but no I just thought – is, there's no option for her so I might as well keep more of it.

UNIT 8 Recording 5

J = Jim   L = Liz

J: Here's your coffee.

L: Thanks, Jim. Oh, I needed that.

J: No problem. Hey, Liz, there's something I've been meaning to talk to you about.

L: Oh yeah?

J: It's just that … well … you know you borrowed some money from me last week?

L: Oh, right. It was ten euros, wasn't it? I don't actually have that on me at the moment.

J: It's not that, it's … I hope you don't take this the wrong way, but, um …

L: Right.

J: … it's just that this isn't the first time I've lent you money and er, well you haven't paid it back. I mean, I know it's not a lot, just small amounts each time but it kind of adds up quite quickly … I dunno. Do you know what I mean?

L: Yeah. Sorry. I didn't realise. I know I'm terrible with money. I just forget. Look, I promise I'll give it back, but could you wait a week? Until I get paid.

J: Well, actually, you've said that once before. I don't want you to get the wrong idea, but … it, you know, never happened. And it makes things slightly awkward. It makes me feel just a bit annoyed. Do you see where I'm coming from?

L: Oh. Yeah. I suppose so.

J: Look, I've got a suggestion. I'd feel better if we could work out how much is owed and then you could pay me back a little each week, you know, however much you can afford. How does that sound?

L: Yeah, yeah. That sounds reasonable.

J: OK, great so …

UNIT 8 Recording 8

OK, here are some things that I think would be useful if you're visiting the States, especially if you're coming here to do business.

So first of all, with names. When you first meet someone, it's considered good manners to use a title along with their surname, you know like Mr Smith or Ms Jones, and so on. But the funny thing is that in fact people will in most cases want to use first names, you know be on a first-name basis, like 'Hey call me "Bob"' and all that. That might not be comfortable for you but in fact if you stick to a more formal Mr Smith sort of thing, it's not going to be comfortable for them. I also think that once they know your name you'll find people use it a lot, so they'll say it periodically in a conversation. If you're not used to it, it can seem strange at first.

Now with meeting people for the first time … It's pretty normal for people to shake hands, or at least guys do. Women usually do, certainly in business, but not always. On the whole, Americans tend to avoid greetings that involve hugging and other close physical contact, except with family members and friends. Having said that, don't be surprised if someone gives you a hug the first time you meet them, either as a hello or a goodbye. You sort of have to keep your eyes open and try to anticipate what they'll do.

When people sit down, like in a meeting, people like to get comfortable, so people cross their legs with one ankle on the other knee. I know this is rude in some countries but it's normal here. That reminds me, if you're chatting with someone in an office, standing up, they might sit on a desk, which I know is a big no-no in places like Japan. Other gestures? Well, if an American wants to show agreement, they'll sometimes give the thumbs up sign or they'll make a circle out of their thumb and index finger. Don't be offended if in your culture this isn't polite. It just means 'A OK' in the States.

Last of all, timing: punctuality is very important for business occasions and it's unacceptable to be late, and if you are late it will be appreciated if you let your contact know if you are going to be late. It's the same for social occasions, you need to arrive on time.

Of course, having said all this, it's important to remember that the United States is huge and there's a lot of variety in what's acceptable in different places. Anyway, I hope this advice helps.

UNIT 9 Recording 2

Conversation 1

L = Lise   J = Jeff

L: So what happened was, I was sitting in a café and this young couple – they looked like tourists – asked me to take a photo of them. And I took their photo, and they thanked me and left and then I looked at my seat and realised my handbag had gone, with my mobile, wallet, credit card, keys, everything.

J: No! What did you do?

L: Well, there was a guy on the next table and he saw I was really upset and I explained about the bag and he asked me which bank I was with and he said he worked for that bank and gave me a phone number and let me use his mobile to phone them and stop my credit card.

J: And you believed him?

L: Yeah, I mean I was in a real panic. I was really grateful for his help. Anyway, I phoned the number and talked to a woman from 'the bank' and gave her my name and address and my account number.

J: She sounded genuine?

L: Yeah, completely. I could hear the sounds of the call centre behind her. And she asked me to key in my PIN on the phone and she said they'd stop my card.

J: Wow. And you did? You punched in your PIN?

L: Yeah, unfortunately.

J: So it was a double scam. They got your bag and your bank account details.

L: I felt so stupid.

J: So who actually took your bag?

L: Well, it can't have been the young couple because I was looking at them all the time I was taking the photo. Their job was just to distract me. So it must have been stolen when I was taking the photo.

J: Was it the guy at the next table, then? The fake banker?

L: I think so. He must have taken my bag when I wasn't looking. Then he could have hidden it in his case or maybe he gave it to another member of the gang.

J: And then he gave you a fake phone number to call the bank.

L: Yeah, and they probably used a recording of a call centre so that it sounded like the real bank.

Conversation 2

D = Dan   I = Ingrid

D: I was badly tricked a few years ago when I was working in a jewellery shop.

I: You never told me about that. What happened?

D: Well, this woman came in and was looking at necklaces. She was young, attractive, well dressed, and then a guy came in shortly afterwards and he was just looking around. But then the woman went to pay for a very expensive necklace that she'd picked out, and when she was counting out the money onto the counter, the guy grabbed her, flashed his police ID and said he was arresting her for paying with counterfeit money.

I: Fake money! Wow!

D: So he took the cash and the necklace as evidence, wrote down his contact details, and promised me he'd bring the necklace back by the end of the day. I didn't suspect anything. Then he took the woman away, presumably to book her at the police station.

I: And he didn't come back?

D: No, and stupid me, I didn't even begin to suspect anything until it was closing time, so then I phoned the police and they had no idea what I was talking about. That was it, end of story.

I: How much was the necklace worth?

D: £600. And my boss took it out of my salary. That's why I quit.

I: So the police ID was a fake.

D: Must have been. I just didn't check it.

I: And wait a second, was the woman a real customer?

D: No, the woman must have been working with the guy. She couldn't have been a real customer or she wouldn't have gone with him …

I: But she might have had fake money.

D: I really don't think so.

I: Talk about an ingenious scam …

UNIT 9 Recording 5

P = Police officer   A = Alain

P: Hello, police. Can I help you?

A: Yes, I'd like to report a crime. I've been robbed.

P: I'm very sorry to hear that, Sir. OK, I'll need to take a statement.

A: A statement?

P: To write down some details, if that's all right.

A: Yes, sure.

P: Could you give me your name please, Sir?

A: Alain Girard.

P: Right. That's Girard with a J?

A: No, G, and it's Alain spelled A-l-a-i-n.

P: Right, Mr Girard. Could you tell me exactly when the incident happened?

A: Just now. About an hour ago.

P: Could you be more precise?

A: Excuse me?

P: Could you give me the exact time?

A: I think at 2.50 or 2.55.

P: That's about 2.50 on the seventh of June. And where did it happen?

A: Park Avenue.

P: Can you pinpoint the exact location?

A: Pinpoint?

P: Tell me exactly where.

A: Oh. It was near the entrance to the park. Just about fifty metres inside.

P: OK. Could you tell me what happened?

A: I was walking out of the park, and a man was running towards me and he hit into me hard –

P: He collided with you?

A: Yes and he said 'sorry' and something else, then before I realised what had happened, he had run on. It was only about thirty seconds later that I realised my wallet had gone and that he must have taken it when he hit me, collided with me.

P: But did it cross your mind that it wasn't just an accident?

A: No, it never occurred to me that he'd done it on purpose.

P: Did you run after him?

A: No, my mind just went blank and I stood there not knowing what to do.

P: But you were OK? Not hurt?

A: No, just very shocked.

P: OK. Could you tell me exactly what your wallet looked like and what was in it?

A: It's brown leather and it has my credit card and about 250 euros and –

P: Hold on a minute, credit card … about 250 euros, yes?

A: And a photo of my girlfriend.

P: OK. So you saw the man. Can you give me a description?

A: Erm, about twenty, white, quite tall. And he was wearing a sweater, grey colour with a … you know … erm, something you put over your head …

P: A hood? He was wearing a hoodie?

A: Yes, that's the word. So I didn't see his face, not clearly. But he looked as if he was just out jogging, you know, he was wearing some sort of dark trousers, for running or for the gym.

P: Tracksuit bottoms?

A: Yeah. I can't remember anything else, it all happened so quickly.

P: So that's a tall white male, about twenty, wearing a grey hoodie and dark tracksuit bottoms?

A: That's right.

P: And did he have any other distinguishing marks or features?

A: Sorry?

P: Anything special or different from normal? For example, a scar on his face or anything like that?

A: No, he just seemed like a normal guy, out running. Nothing special. Except …

P: Yes?

A: He reminded me a bit of that actor, Vin Diesel. But younger. Do you know who I mean?

P: Vin Diesel, yeah. I'll put it down. And you said he said something to you.

A: Yeah, but I didn't catch what he said. It was too quick.

P: Right, one last question and then I'll take your contact details. Were there any other people in the vicinity?

A: Vicinity?

P: In the surrounding area – nearby. Any witnesses who saw what had happened?

A: No, there was no one nearby, in the … vicinity.

P: Right, now I just need to take your contact details, Mr Girard, and I can also give you a phone number to ring if …

UNIT 9 Recording 8

W1 = Woman 1   M = Man   W2 = Woman 2

W1: So, we really need to decide then what it is we get rid of and what is absolutely essential to keep on the life raft, I think that's probably the most important thing, isn't it?

M: I'm sure it's easy to get rid of a few things, isn't it?

W2: Like what?

M: Well, I'm not sure about the lighter. I mean, we can't really start a fire on a raft, can we?

W2: No.

W1: I suppose it depends on what the life raft is made out of, doesn't it?

M: Yeah, but it's not exactly top priority to be able to cook a hot meal, you know, when you really just need to survive.

W1: So no lighter?

M and W2: OK.

W1: OK. So what do you think is important?

W2: I'd say that a blanket is essential.

W1: Interesting choice. What for?

W2: Well, you can use it for a lot of different things. To keep you warm obviously, but you can use a blanket as a towel if you get wet –

W1: If you fall in the water.

W2: … for example. And a blanket can protect you from the sun.

M: That hadn't occurred to me. OK, I'm convinced. So what else?

W1: Well I can't see the point of taking the hand mirror can you?

M: Actually, I can. Because if …

UNIT 10 Recording 1

A: So come on then, favourite movie of all time.

B: Um, I would have to say, cos I love action films, uh, that it would be *Speed* – have you ever seen that?

A: *Speed*?

B: Yeah it's with Keanu Reeves and Sandra Bullock.

A: Oh, I like her.

B: She's very good isn't she? Um, so yeah, I just love any kind of action film. And I remember watching it when I was really young and watching it with my dad. And it's the sort of, like, a family-friendly action film, because it's not too violent, it's not too gory but it's just really tense. And I remember just like watching it, we had a cushion, me and my dad, and I was just like what's gonna happen next? Um, have you seen it?

A: No! I haven't I, I think I've seen bits of it, like trailers and things but …

B: OK, it's um …

A: No, I knew she was in it.

B: Yeah, so basically, he, uh, there's a baddy in it, as every action film it has a good baddy, and he's got no thumb. I remember that, that was like a memorable bit of it, he had no thumb. And so they sort of highjack this … this bus. And it's set that it can only drive at a certain speed – hence the name. And so it's just basically driving through,

through the city and it can't stop otherwise there's a bomb and it's gonna blow it up. Um, so, and there's a, Keanu Reeves he's, um, he's the goody he's uh a policeman. And he's … he jumps on board the bus to try and stop this bomb from going off. And, uh, it's just all the different characters on the bus. It's just really …

A: The whole film is on the bus?

B: Yeah and, but it's, it's, well not at the beginning, it sort of goes onto the bus. But uh, it's just I remember it being so tense and gripping, 'cos you just didn't know what was gonna happen. You didn't know.

A: It sounds really uncomfortable to watch, was it not?

B: It … it's … I just like that kind of that feeling of like pure suspense 'cos you just have no idea if it's gonna end well or not. And it did end very well. You have to watch it.

A: Well yeah, as long as there's, you know, a point when you can relax, 'cos I don't like feeling like that the whole way through a movie, anxiety.

B: Yeah, because you know when it's like driving along, and it, 'cos I think it has to stay at fifty miles per hour. And uh, so uh, if there's, driving along a motorway and it's, there's traffic and stuff you have to change the route and things, so you just don't know where its gonna go.

A: Oh, OK.

B: And then they get to a bridge that's um, hasn't finished being built. Uh so you're not sure how they're gonna get over the bridge and stuff like that. So there's lots of moments where you just think, I have no clue what's gonna happen.

A: Good stunts?

B: Very good, and I heard that he did all his stunts himself, Keanu Reeves.

A: Yes, they always say that.

B: He likes a bit of action, doesn't he? So, and I think it always helps to have a very good heroine in a film and she's, she's beautiful, don't you think?

A: Yes, I love her. I think she's very funny, but tell me there's some comedy in there.

B: Um, there's not a huge amount of comedy. Uh, it's one of your traditional sort of American blockbuster action films. So yeah but it's, it's just, it's – there's not many action films with comedy in though are there?

A: I think that's why I don't watch them.

B: Oh really?

A: Yeah.

B: What's your sort of, your favourite type of film?

A: I don't like to feel uncomfortable so it's just comedy.

B: Watch *Speed*.

A: Mm mm OK.

UNIT 10 Recording 5

Conversation 1

W = Woman   M = Man

W: So here we are in Greenwich Village.

M: It looks very different from the rest of New York.

W: Yeah, the streets are quite narrow and the buildings aren't as high.

M: It does look quite village-like.

W: Yeah, but it's quite big. It extends out west that way to the Hudson River, north above Washington Square. We'll go up there in a bit.

M: And you lived here?

W: When I first came to New York, yeah. In an apartment just around the corner, on West Third Street. Actually, you can see the building over there.

M: Near The Blue Note Jazz Club?

W: Yeah.

M: I've heard of The Blue Note.

W: It's pretty famous. There are some great jazz clubs around the neighbourhood, and that's one of the best. We can see a show there one night if you want.

M: That'd be great.

W: Now up here on the left is the Café Reggio. It's where I used to hang out and read when I wasn't working.

M: Looks good.

W: Their cappuccino is great. The story goes that the original owner brought cappuccino to America. You can see the original cappuccino machine inside.

M: Cool. We could stop and have a coffee.

W: Maybe a bit later? Let's head over to Washington Square Park and then circle back.

M: OK – lead the way!

…

W: A lot of these clubs we're walking by have a real history. As I'm sure you know, Greenwich Village has always been a centre of artistic life – very bohemian. It's always attracted famous writers, dancers and poets. And in the sixties, it was a big part of the folk music scene: Simon and Garfunkel, Joni Mitchell, Bob Dylan, you know.

M: Before my time! Now what's this?

W: This is Washington Square Park. We'll walk into the park on this side. Can you play chess?

M: A bit, yeah.

W: Any of these guys here would be happy to challenge you to a game of chess. They're here all day, every day.

M: Maybe next time – I'm not that good! What's the arch over there? It looks like the Arc de Triomphe in Paris.

W: Well it should, that's the Washington Square arch. It was modelled on the Arc de Triomphe and built in 1889 to celebrate the hundredth anniversary of the inauguration of George Washington as president.

M: Could we sit down a second? I need a break.

W: Why don't we retrace our steps and go back to the Café Reggio?

M: Sounds good. I could really do with a coffee.

Conversation 2

M1 = Man 1   W = Woman   M2 = Man 2

M1: So, this is Radcliffe Square.

W: Wow! Is this right in the centre then?

M1: Pretty much.

M2: What's that?

M1: Hold on. Let's just get off our bikes … Right, so that building in front of us is the Bodleian, named after the founder – Thomas Bodley. Believe it or not, despite the fact that it's circular, it's actually a library.

W: Cool!

M1: Yeah, it gets a copy of every book published in the UK.

M2: Who can use it?

M1: Any student at the university. Of course, each college also has its own library – you know the university's divided into colleges, right?

M2: Right. How many colleges are there?

M1: Just under forty. Well, thirty-eight to be exact.

W: So that means thirty-eight libraries?!

M1: Mm but they're not all as big as the Bodleian. Anyway, we'll need to get back on our bikes for the next bit.

…

M1: Can you hear me if I talk as we cycle along?

M2: Yeah.

W: OK, but don't go too fast. I'm not very steady on this thing!

M1: So, here's the famous Bridge of Sighs, connecting two sides of Hertford College.

M2: I've seen the original.

M1: What, of the bridge? In Italy, you mean?

M2: Ja, it's in Venice. Beautiful.

M1: OK. We'll go past New College and then onto the High Street.

M2: Is that New College there?

M1: Yep.

W: How 'new' is new?

M1: Roughly 1370.

W: You're kidding!

M1: No, really! Interestingly, the oldest college was actually only founded a hundred or so years earlier! Uh-oh, watch out on this corner …

M1: That's the 'Schools'. It's where the students take their exams. Apparently, the biggest room can seat somewhere in the region of 500 students although I haven't seen it myself. Anyway, we're turning right here. The street's cobbled, so be careful.

M2: How many students are there at the university in total?

M1: To be honest, it depends. In term time, you'd probably get upwards of 20,000.

M2: Many international students?

M1: Some, but most are from the UK. We'll finish by cycling down this way to Christ Church. We can actually go inside if we're quick. It's well worth a visit.

M2: Christ Church is another college?

M1: Yeah, the biggest and probably the most famous. Have you seen any of the Harry Potter films?

M2: No …

W: I have!

M1: Oh, well, you'll recognise the Great Hall. It's where they have the feasts in Hogwarts School. You know that bit when Harry …

AUDIO SCRIPTS

S = Sarah   T = Tim   N = Nigel

S: Right, well, we have our shortlist for the new feature that we're going to put into the town centre, which one gets your vote, Tim?

T: I'm really in favour of the – the state-of-the-art multiplex cinema. I think that it would be most useful and beneficial for the community. I think it will be used a great deal, I think it would bring jobs to the area, and I think it would provide entertainment and activities for young people.

N: The only thing that would concern me though is that that's going to be very, very expensive.

T: Um hm.

S: I mean, I personally would prefer the botanical garden.

T: Oh.

S: Because I think that that will satisfy the needs of many different age groups. I think it would be very good for wheelchairs, for … for blind people, for people with disabilities, there would be areas that would be excellent for young people, and lots of learning opportunities in the education centre. And we know from past experience that the older age group certainly enjoy gardens.

T: The only thing that would concern me on that is that you mention youth, but I don't think that you're going to get as many young people involved in a botanical garden. I think if it was interactive then it would be … but just as a thing that was showing I'm, I'm not so sure.

N: Well, I don't want to harp on about costs again but we have to consider the maintenance of this botanical garden. There are very high maintenance costs involved.

S: Oh, so, Nigel what, what would you prefer?

N: Well, my vote would go to the theatre workshop space for young people. And I know we said we don't want to discriminate against any … we don't want to leave out certain members of our society, but I think we've got a problem in this town about kids getting bored, hanging around on street corners, they need something to do and a theatre workshop space is going to get them … it's going to give them a routine, it's going to give them a motivation, and then when they do their shows, they're bringing along their grandparents, their parents, I feel it's very inclusive.

T: Can you see the older generation wanting it, liking it?

N: I think the older generation want to be sure that kids aren't hanging about the streets with nothing to do.

S: And could that theatre workshop space be used for other things as well?

N: Absolutely.

S: Could it be used for meetings, for other sections of society?

N: … Aerobics … there's going to be a sprung wooden floor so there'll be dance classes, yoga, pilates, multi-purpose …

Pearson Education Limited
Edinburgh Gate
Harlow
Essex CM20 2JE
England
and Associated Companies throughout the world.

www.pearsonelt.com

First published 2015
Fourth impression 2018
ISBN: 978-1-292-16103-7
Set in Aptifer sans 10/12 pt
Printed by CPI UK

Acknowledgements

The Publisher and authors would like to thank the
following people and institutions for their feedback and
comments during the development of the material:
Australia: Erica Lederman; **Hungary:** Eszter Timár;
Poland: Konrad Dejko; **Spain:** Pilar Álvarez Polvorinos,
Victoria O'Dea; **UK:** David Byrne, Lilian Del Gaudio
Maciel, Niva Gunasegaran.

Text acknowledgements

Extract on page 12 adapted from "30 Challenges for
30 Days" by Martijn Schirp, http://www.highexistence.
com/30-challenges-for-30-days. Reproduced by kind
permission of Martijn Schirp; Extract on page 32
adapted from "You Are Wonderful!", *Cultivate Life!*
magazine, Issue 26 (Phil Evans, http://www.peoplestuff.
com.au), http://www.trans4mind.com/cultivate-life-
magazine/issue-026/Regular-Features-page-one.html,
copyright © 1997-2014 Trans4mind Ltd. Reproduced
with permission; Extracts on page 33 adapted from
"What goes around comes around" by Stephen, 18
October 2008, http://academictips.org/blogs/what-
goes-around-comes-around, and "The Falcon & The
Branch" submitted by Hemendra Chanchani, 7 March
2014, http://academictips.org/blogs/the-falcon-and-
the-branch. Reproduced with permission; Extract
on page 35 adapted from Today (feature on 'Life in
six words') by host Sarah Montague and guest Larry
Smith, 28/06/2007, http://www.bbc.co.uk/radio4/today/
reports/misc/sixwordlife_20080205.shtml, copyright
© BBC Worldwide Limited; Extracts on pages 37, 44,
70, 107, 121, from *Longman Active Study Dictionary*, 5th
edition, Pearson Education Ltd, copyright © Pearson
Education Limited, 2010; Extract on page 71 adapted
from 'Letters to myself', 22/02/2009, Audio interview
on BBC Radio 4 copyright © BBC Worldwide Limited;
Extract on page 86 adapted from 'Six topics that keep
the tabloids in business', http://www.drewrys.com,
copyright © John Drewry; Extract on page 92 adapted
from "New York roommates find $40,000 in sofa and
return cash to owner", *Associated Press*, 16/05/2014,
copyright © 2105. Reproduced with permission of The
Associated Press. All rights reserved; Extract on page
92 adapted from "Unemployed Brooklyn man misses
job interview to save 9-month-old boy who was blown
into path of oncoming subway train", *New York Daily
News*, 27/06/2012 (Kerry Burke, Joe Kemp and Tracy
Connor), copyright © Daily News, L.P. (New York).
Used with permission; and Extract on pages 104-105
from "Memories on Trial" by Andy Ridgway, *BBC Focus*,
January 2009, pp.58–61, copyright © Immediate Media
Company Bristol Ltd.

Illustration acknowledgements

Fred Blunt: 18, 90, 150, 153, 155; Lyndon Hayes: 161, 162;
Eric Smith: 156; Mark Willey: 107; Mariko Yamazaki: 72,
159.

Photo acknowledgements

The Publisher would like to thank the following for their
kind permission to reproduce their photographs:

(Key: b-bottom; c-centre; l-left; r-right; t-top)

123RF.com: Arcady31 15t, Belchonock 92cr, Robert
Churchill 55cr, 62, Iakov Kalinin 52-53b, Katre 15tc,
Andrey Kiselev 99cl, Maska82 91cl, Igor Mojzes 151 (f),
Kathawut Rueansai 12, Andrei Shumskiy 7b (icon), 19b
(icon), 31b (icon), 43b (icon), 55b (icon), 67b (icon),
79b (icon), 91b (icon), 103b (icon), 115b (icon), Сергей
Тряпицын 43l, 44cr; **Alamy Images:** Adam Burton 40-
41b, Age Fotostock 86-87t, Ammentorp Photography
110b, Art Directors & Trip 38tr, 55r, 64-65b, 152 (f),
Ben Molyneux 38 (Life of Pi), Blend Images 311, CBW
38 (The Hunger Games), 38 (The Kite Runner), Judith
Collins 87cl, Caroline Cortizo 71, Cultura Creative 99tl,
Design Pics Inc 36bl, Dorling Kindersley ltd 119b, Chuck
Eckert 156, Mark Harvey 19cl, 24, Image Source 79r,
James Callaghan 58 (d), Keystone Pictures USA 69
(5), Marka 69 (1), Newscast 152 (e), Ben Nicholson
123 (e), Dale O'Dell 79cl, Pacific Press Service 67r,
76-77, PhotoAlto 74l, Pictorial Press Ltd 69 (4), Rafael
Ben-Ari 67l, 70, Paul Rapson 95, Redsnapper 39cl, Ros
Drinkwater 121b, Ross Gilmore 47c, Alistair Scott 162,
Adrian Sherratt 149 (a), Marmaduke St. John 122 (b),
Stocksearch 35 (car), Glyn Thomas 32tl, 158c, Maximilian
Weinzierl 11tr, WENN Ltd 59br, Tim Whitby 103cl,
ZUMA Press, Inc. 69 (2); **Ardea:** Thomas Marent 16tl;
BBC Photo Library: Laurence Cendrowicz 31r, 40br,
Rod Fountain 81b, Guy Levy 81tl, Jeff Overs 88-89b,
Adrian Rogers 80br; **BBC Worldwide Ltd:** 28cl, 40cl,
52bl, 64l, 76, 88cl, 100cl, 112cl; **Corbis:** 167 / Ocean /
Alex Treadway 43cl, Markus Altmann 91t, Ed Bock
98tr, Cardinal 11cr, Dpa / Marius Becker 23t, Monalyn
Gracia 43t, 47bc, Henglein and Steets 8tl, David Sacks
82, Wavebreak Media Ltd 91cr; **Digital Vision:** 91cr; **DK
Images:** Dorling Kindersley 89 (snow globe); **Endemol
UK:** 43r, 50-51t; **Exclusivepix:** 83 (a); **Eyewire:** 157
(c), Eyewire 157 (k); **Fotolia.com:** albphoto 122 (d),
artzenter 58 (c), Bergamont 152 (a), Markus Bormann
152 (b), Diego Cervo 63t, Chones 55t, Christopher
Dodge 57l, Timo Darco 26tr, Esebene 3lcl, Gajus 67cl,
Georgerudy 151 (e), Kletr 57cl, Markus Mainka 58 (b),
Martincp 63l, Mediagram 58l, Photomelon 89 (paperclip),
Pioneer11 60, Piotr Adamowicz 56c, Production Perig
15tr, Rawpixel 15, Rebius 83 (plane), Savoieleysse
106, Sentello 56r, Sergemi 83 (Man hanging on rope),
Trekandphoto 16tr, Winston 55cl, 59l, Xuejun li 152 (c);
Getty Images: Ablestock.com 157 (j), Archive Photos
35tl, AWL Images / Nigel Pavitt 19l, 20tl, Blend Images /
Stewart Cohen / Pam Ostrow 148 (a), Leland Bobbe
115l, Christopher Bierlein 122 (c), Cynthia Johnson 69
(3), E+ / Nikada 25c, E+ / Sjharmon 98tc, Don Farrall
92bl, FilmMagic / Shareif Ziyadat 37tr, Stephen Frink
16-17b, Christopher Furlong 124bl, Craig Holmes 115r,
124-125, Imagebroker / Uwe Umstatter 27tr, Daniel
Ingold / RF 115cr, iStock / mamadela 35tc, Jupiter images
20cr, Carsten Koall 83 (flooded house), Rich Legg
105, Martha Holmes 58 (a), Stijn Nieuwendijk 8tr, 8cl,
Photodisc / Arne Pastoor 94, Photodisc / James Lauritz
19t, Photolibrary / Spencer Grant 149 (b), Popperfoto
57r, Joe Raedle / Staff 115t, Dmitriy Shironosov 20tr,
Stocktrex 103r, 112-113b, William Casey 67cr, 75, Alena
Yakusheva 19r, 28-29b; **Gulf Images:** 148 (b); **Hartwood
Films:** Hartwood Films 81tc; **Imagemore Co., Ltd:**
108, 157 (b), 157 (h), 157 (i); **Nature Picture Library:**
Eric Baccega 79l, 80tr; **Pearson Education Ltd:** Steve
Shott 27tl; **PhotoDisc:** Tony Gable. C Squared Studios
157 (g), McDaniel Woolf 126, **Rex Features:** 51tl, 104,
Endemol UK 50tl, Kevin Holt / Daily Mail 69 (6), Mark
Large 121t, Geoffrey Robinson 79t, Karl Schoendorfer
38-39cl; **Robert Harding World Imagery:** Jose Azel
47br, Jens Lucking 43cr, 47tr, Philippe Michel 48-49t;
Shutterstock.com: Fabio Alcini 152 (d), Steve Allen 123
(f), amenic181 74bc, Arena Creative 15tl, Awe Inspiring
Images 7t, 16c, Galina Barskaya 84, Beboy 149 (d),
Bikeriderlondon 97, Natalia Bratslavsky 91l, 92tr, Jakub
Cejpek 154bc, Christian Bertrand 115cl, Christophe
Testi 89 (doorknob), Creatista 74r, De Visu 109, Goran
Djukanovic 119t, Furtseff 157 (f), Icsnaps 151 (a), Iofoto
149 (c), Italianestro 157 (e), Jill Battaglia 35 (money),
Julian Rovagnati 63r, Anna Jurkovska 31cr, Kachalkina
Veronika 73l, Deborah Kolb 83 (shark fins), kornilov007
103cr, 110t, Sergey Krasnoshchokov 7r, 16tc, Piotr

Krzeslak 103l, Labrador Photo Video 59tr, Liligraphie 67t,
Isantilli 151 (c), Mangostock 19cr, Marie C Fields 34b,
Minerva Studio 79cr, nanhatai 74tc, Nejron Photo 7cl,
11tl, Vitalii Nesterchuk 11tc, 16cr, Nito 47tc, Nneirda
154br, Jakkrit Orrasri 151 (d), Bombaert Patrick 157 (d),
Pressmaster 9br, Primopiano 56l, Rawpixel 100-101b,
Dario Sabljak 157 (l), Sabphoto 148 (c), scyther5 55l,
57cr, Stockelements 122 (a), TFoxFoto 103t, Toa55 33tr,
158br, Tatyana Vyc 151 (b), wavebreakmedia 71, Ivonne
Wierink 157 (a), Zvonimir Atletic 73r; **SuperStock:**
31t, Blend Images 7cr, Fancy Collection 85; **The Kobal
Collection:** 20th Century Fox 116t, Columbia /
Tri-Star / Goldman, Louis 116b, Gravier Productions
118; **The Orion Publishing Group Ltd:** Cover Design
Orionbooks, Image © Bernd Ott / Gallerystock 38
(Gone Girl)

All other images © Pearson Education